IMAGES
OF
CIVIL WAR
MEDICINE

A PHOTOGRAPHIC HISTORY

D1595100

IMAGES
OF
CIVIL WAR MEDICINE

A PHOTOGRAPHIC HISTORY

Containing Numerous Previously
Unpublished Photographs of Surgeons, Nurses,
Hospitals, and Other Facilities Used During the Civil War

Gordon E. Dammann, DDS
Alfred Jay Bollet, MD

ABOUT THE COVER: The cover picture illustrates a little-known fact about Civil War surgery, that a group of three consulting surgeons made the decision about whether to amputate. The consulting surgeons are seen examining a wounded soldier while another surgeon stands by holding a knife, ready to operate if necessary. Consultations such as this were required by order of Dr. Jonathan Letterman, Medical Director of the Army of the Potomac, beginning in the fall of 1862, in order to prevent unnecessary amputations. Later it was required throughout the Union Army and a similar procedure was adopted by Confederate armies. The picture was taken at Gettysburg. See page 170.

Special discounts on bulk quantities of Demos Medical Publishing books are available to corporations, professional associations, pharmaceutical companies, health care organizations, and other qualifying groups. For details, please contact:

Special Sales Department
DEMOS MEDICAL PUBLISHING
386 Park Avenue South, Suite 301
New York, NY 10016
Telephone: 800-532-8663 or 212-683-0072
Fax: 212-683-0118
Email: orderdept@demosmedpub.com

Visit our website at www.demosmedpub.com

LIBRARY OF CONGRESS CATALOGING-IN-PUBLICATION DATA

Dammann, Gordon.
Images of Civil War medicine: a photographic history / Gordon E. Dammann,
Alfred Jay Bollet.
p. ; cm.
Includes bibliographical references and index.
ISBN-13: 978-1-932603-39-2 (alk. paper)
ISBN-10: 1-932603-39-5 (alk. paper)
1. United States—History—Civil War, 1861–1865—Medical care—Pictorial works.
2. Medicine, Military—United States—History—19th century—Pictorial works.
3. Dammann, Gordon—Photograph collections.   4. National Museum of Civil War
Medicine—Photograph collections.   I. Bollet, Alfred J.   II. Title.
[DNLM: 1. Military Medicine—History—United States—Pictorial Works.
2. American Civil War—United States—Pictorial Works.   E 621 D162i   2008] E621.D36   2008
973.7'75—dc22
2007029463

Book design by Steven Pisano

MADE IN THE UNITED STATES OF AMERICA

07 08 09 10   5 4 3 2 1

CONTENTS

PREFACE

ESPITE POPULAR MYTHS TO THE CONTRARY, the medical care received by soldiers of the Civil War measured up to the international standards of the time, and many important advances were made during the course of the war. Students of the war have documented the efforts of the physicians, the quality of care given, and the advances made, based on contemporary records. Although it was quite new, photography became very popular during the Civil War. As a result, a vast array of pictures is available to us, allowing the illustration of many of the medical events and experiences of the time.

The authors have been very interested in the events of the Civil War, arguably the most important historical event of the nineteenth century for Americans. In addition to studying the events and records of the war, Dr. Gordon Dammann has been collecting Civil War memorabilia since 1972. After the collection grew to almost 4,000 items, the idea of a museum devoted to the subject developed. After a great deal of effort, the National Museum of Civil War Medicine was founded in 1992 in Frederick, Maryland. The museum, which formally opened to the public in 1996, was the first to be devoted to the medical events of the years 1861 to 1865. Dr. Dammann has also written three books on the medical instruments and equipment of that era,[1] and has lectured widely on the subject.

Images were not the original focus of Dr. Dammann's collection. But because of the importance of the visual images of war events, his collection expanded to include pictures that told the story of Civil War medicine. He enjoyed finding unpublished photos of surgeons, nurses, hospitals, and other scenes that helped illustrate the story. Although books have been written on some aspect or another of the Civil War seemingly at the rate of one a day since the war ended, relatively little has been written about medicine during the war. Other than the official publications of the Surgeon General's Office immediately after the war, only one other book—one devoted to orthopedic injuries[2] —includes images of Civil War medicine.

The other member of our team, Dr. Alfred Jay Bollet—a physician and professor of medicine—is also a lifelong student of the war. His investigations of the records of Civil War medical events led to the publication of a book that won the Writing Award of the Army Historical Foundation for 2002, and he has lectured widely on the subject.[3]

From the collaboration of these two authors, this book came into being. It describes the major features of the medical experiences of the war, and it is the first book to make extensive use of images to tell what Civil War medicine was all about. Most of the images—especially the visiting cards (*cartes de visite*) so popular at the time, featuring pictures of Civil War surgeons—have never been published before. More than 400 general hospitals, which operated in existing buildings or in facilities hastily built for the purpose, were put into service during the war. Many images of these institutions, most never published previously, are included in this book. These hospitals were a major innovation of the war. Such military hospitals had not existed previously, and relatively few civilian hospitals were in operation. As John Shaw Billings wrote, "We taught Europe how to build, organize and run hospitals."[4] The images of these institutions add immeasurably to the records of the war.

We would like to acknowledge the assistance of the people who helped us in this endeavor, especially Drs. Terry Hambrecht, T. Adrian Wheat, and Jonathan O'Neal for providing some of the images; Karen Dammann; and the staffs of Demos Medical Publishing and the National Museum of Civil War Medicine. Dr. Dammann would also like to thank Jeri Strohecker, Larry Nelson, Don McNabb, and Gary Albright for their help.

ENDNOTES

1 Dammann, G., *Pictorial Encyclopedia of Civil War Medical Instruments and Equipment*, Vol I, Vol II, Vol III. Missoula, Mont., Pictorial Histories Publishing Company, 1983 (Vol I), 1988 (Vol II), 1998 (Vol III).

2 Kuz, J.F., and Bengston, B.P., *Orthopedic Injuries of the Civil War*, Kennesaw, Ga., Kennesaw Mountain Press, 1996.

3 Bollet, A.J., *Civil War Medicine, Challenges and Triumphs*, Galen Press, Tucson, Ariz., 2002.

4 Billings, J.S., in Barnes, J.K., *Medical and Surgical History of the War of the Rebellion*, Washington, D.C., Surgeon General's Office, 1870–1888.

IMAGES
OF
CIVIL WAR
MEDICINE

A PHOTOGRAPHIC HISTORY

INTRODUCTION:

THE DEVELOPMENT

OF PHOTOGRAPHY

AND ITS APPLICATION

TO MEDICINE

MODERN MEDICINE RELIES GREATLY ON IMAGING. The use of X-ray, MRI, CAT scans, telemetry, photography, TV, and the sonogram and echogram help diagnose and treat disease. Many people are not aware that medical imagery started during the American Civil War (1861–65). This period was the first time that images were taken of war wounds and anatomical specimens to help instruct medical personnel. One of the pioneers of medical imagery was Dr. Reed Bontecou, who worked in Harewood Hospital in Washington, D.C. He was responsible for having many war injuries photographed. Soon after the war was over, many of these images were published in the six volumes of *The Medical and Surgical History of the War of Rebellion*, a work that would be recognized worldwide for its contribution of knowledge of war wounds and diseases and their treatments. In order to understand imagery during the Civil War, it is necessary to look to the years leading up to 1861.

Many say that Louis-Jacques Mandé Daguerre was the father of photography. However, Jean-Louis Marignier writes in the *Daguerreian Annual* (2002–2003) that "J. Nicéphore Niépce is known for the invention of the photographic process, which, in 1824, allowed him to obtain the first permanent photographs in the world. For this he deserves the title of inventor of photography. In 1829, he entered into partnership with Louis-Jacques Mandé Daguerre, an association that ended with the death of Niépce in 1833."

Niépce called his invention "heliography." The process required a silver plate (a plate of highly polished silver), on which was placed a solution of asphalt (bitumen of Judea) dissolved in oil of lavender. The solution evaporated. After exposure to light, the image was brought forth, again using oil of lavender with white petroleum. The image was reversed using iodine vapors.[1] To learn more about this process, the *Daguerreian Annual* (2002–2003) is a fine source of information.

In 1839, Louis-Jacques Mandé Daguerre invented the process known as the "daguerreotype." Some of the most beautiful and intricate of all photographic images were made using this process. Even today, with all of our digital photography, modern images pale compared to an exquisitely produced daguerreotype. In his process, Daguerre used a copper plate coated with silver. This plate was highly polished and made sensitive to light by the addition of iodine. This image was exposed using a camera. "To bring out the image the silver surface was fumed with mercury vapor, which was then washed in a fixing bath to remove any unexposed silver salts. The resulting image was a direct positive. Since there was no negative, each plate was unique."[2]

Ambrotype photograph of unknown Union soldier.

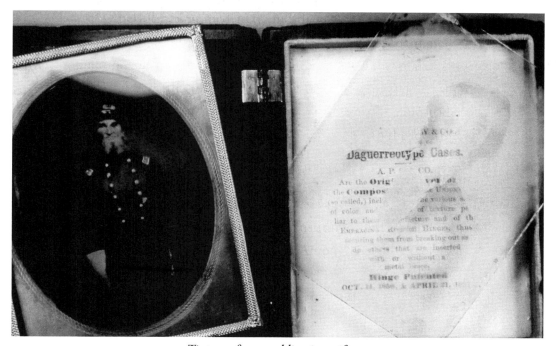

Tintype of same soldier, in uniform.

Ivory-type photo of Surg. William Hayes, of the 28th Massachusetts, with his niece.

Daguerreotype plates are found in various sizes: the half plate measures 4¼" × 5½"; the quarter plate measures 3¼" × 4¼"; and the sixth plate measures 2¾" × 3¼". These plates are very delicate and are susceptible to tarnish, so they were placed in a sealed package with glass in the front and a leather, paper, or thermoplastic (gutta-percha) case to protect them. The cases are a work of art in themselves. It is important to remember that the daguerreotype is a highly polished silver support and that the quality of appearing as a positive or negative therefore depends on the direction of the light that falls on it.

The cost of a daguerreotype image at the time of the Civil War could be as high as five dollars, which was very expensive. Some of the images were tinted with color, which was a combination of pigment and gum arabic; hence "miniature paintings" came about. "The heyday of the 'mirror with the memory,' as Oliver Wendell Holmes described the glowing miniatures, ended in this country in the late 1850s."[3]

The next stage in the progress of early photography was the development of an image called the "ambrotype." This also is a positive image on a nonpaper support. The ambrotype had glass as its support. For the image, "there was a physically developed silver image in a collodion binder on an opaque, nonreflective support. The lightest parts of the images have the most silver and the darkest parts have none. . . . In reflected light, these images have a characteristic creamy whitish appearance, because their silver image particles are the right size and shape to scatter light back to the eye, rather than absorbing the light to make the image appear black. The more silver present in a given area, the whiter the image looks."[4] This process was cheaper than the daguerreotype, but it also required a case because of its fragility. The ambrotype was in use from 1855 to 1865.

The next process, similar to the ambrotype, was the "tintype." Again, it was a positive image on a nonpaper support. The support for this process was iron. It should perhaps have been called the "ferrotype" or "melanotype," but it was known as tintype. As with the ambrotype, there is a silver image on a collodion border. These tintypes were very popular during the Civil War because their cost was more reasonable and they were not as delicate as daguerreotypes. Many were cased to protect them from humidity, which caused them to rust. The tintype process was used into the 1930s. By using a strong magnet, one can determine whether a cased image is a true tintype because the iron will be attracted to the magnet.

All of these processes were direct positive images with no negatives; a multiple-lens camera was used to form the images, usually making four images.

Ambrotype of Union surgeon, in Civil War uniform but with 1841 medical officer's sword.

About the same time that Daguerre was working on his process in the 1830s, William Fox Talbot was trying to make images on paper. He knew that silver compounds darken when exposed to light. "Talbot's essential contribution was to identify silver chloride as the silver compound most suitable for photographic printing, and to discover how to use it most effectively."[5] His process used three ingredients: a sheet of fine paper, sodium chloride (salt), and silver nitrate. In the process, the paper was saturated with sodium chloride solution and dried. The sheet was then immersed or coated with silver nitrate. This chemical process formed silver chloride, which was light sensitive. The sensitized paper was exposed to sunlight for a time, and an image appeared with no developing required. Images of leaves and lace were placed directly on the paper, which was then exposed. The name given to the process was "printing out papers."[6]

The next process in the evolution of photography is called the "salt print." Talbot worked to produce a negative with a camera lens. This was done with the introduction of the calotype, or paper-negative process. "Talbot converted photography into a two-step operation involving a negative image with reversed tones from which any number of positive, tonally correct copies could be made. The advantage of the negative/positive approach to photography was that it allowed the easy multiplication of photographic images."[7] The age of relatively inexpensive photography had arrived.

One final process made photography readily available to the masses—the introduction of the albumen print by Louis Evrard in the 1850s. Albumen, composed of beaten and salted egg whites, was applied to salted paper and allowed to dry. This created a new separate layer on which to form the silver image. This allowed the photographer to provide a glossy image that could take on hues of different color.

Most photographers during the Civil War used this process. The most common photographs for the Civil War soldier and, ultimately, for medical imagery were the *cartes de visite* (CDVs)—4" × 2" cards with the images glued to one side. The image was produced by a camera with a movable plate holder, allowing eight to twelve poses to be imprinted on one negative plate. Another factor that lowered the cost for these CDVs was that unskilled laborers could handle the printing process. The price was one dollar for twenty-five CDVs.[8] The photographic "craze" grew, and by the spring of 1860, there were 3,154 photographers in the United States. Almost every soldier, as soon as he was issued a uniform and a weapon, sought out a photographic studio so that his image could be taken and sent home to his loved ones.

Two views of tintype of unindentified Union surgeon.

Tintype photo of unidentified Union surgeon with sword and hat of medical officer.

Mothers, sisters, and girlfriends did the same, so that their beloved soldiers would have their images with them in the field. These were kept by the soldier in a special place, usually in a wallet or in his small Bible, close to his heart. Oliver Wendell Holmes called CDVs the "social currency, the 'sentimental green back' of civilization."[9] The U.S. government saw another use for these popular items—they became revenue producers. The images were taxed: on the reverse side of many CDVs one can find a revenue stamp, which usually cost two or three cents.

The work of large photographic studios, such as Brady, Gardner, and Gibson, brought the horrors of war into the parlors of the home folk. Hours after a battle ended, the photographers descended on the field to capture the carnage. Within days, the images were on display in all the major cities of both the North and the South. The scenes of mangled bodies, corpses, and destroyed homes, hamlets, and cities gave warfare new meaning.

Medical pioneers also saw the importance of photography. Images of wounds and anatomical specimens would become useful teaching tools. The era of medical imagery had begun.

REFERENCES

Coddington, Ronald S. *Faces of the Civil War.* Baltimore and London: The Johns Hopkins University Press, 2004.

Daguerreian Annual. Yearbook of the Daguerreian Society. Pittsburgh, Pa.: The Daguerreian Society, 2002–2003.

Kilgo, Dolores A. *Likeness and Landscape: Thomas M. Easterly and the Art of the Daguerreotype.* St. Louis: Missouri Historical Society Press, 1994.

Reilly, James M. *Care and Identification of 19th Century Photographic Prints*, Rochester, N.Y. Eastman Kodak Books, 1986.

Tintype of unknown Illinois surgeon, possibly Dr. Gordon Dammann.

ENDNOTES

1   The *Daguerreian Annual* 2002–2003, p. 350, article written by Jean-Louis Marignier.

2   Kilgo, Dolores A., *Likeness and Landscape: Thomas M. Easterly and the Art of the Daguerreotype*, p. 2.

3   Ibid, p. 2.

4   Reilly, James M., *Care and Identification of 19th Century Photographic Prints*, p. 51.

5   Ibid, p. 1.

6   Ibid, p. 2.

7   Ibid, p. 2.

8   Coddington, Ronald S., *Faces of the Civil War*, p. xi.

9   Ibid, p. xi.

MEDICAL
EDUCATORS
OF THE
TIME OF
THE CIVIL WAR

THERE ARE AVAILABLE A NUMBER OF PHOTOGRAPHS of prominent medical educators of the antebellum era who played major roles as teachers of the physicians who served in the war. Some also served in senior army positions for at least part of the war.

DR. FRANK HASTINGS HAMILTON

Dr. Frank Hamilton, a leading surgeon in New York City at the time of the Civil War, greatly influenced surgical practice during the war. During the first half of the war, he served in the army himself.

After graduating from Union College in New York in 1830, Hamilton served as an apprentice to a physician and then attended a series of medical lectures at a medical college in Fairfield, New York. After attending the University of Pennsylvania Medical School, he received a formal M.D. degree from that institution in 1835. He became professor of surgery at several medical schools in upstate New York, including the schools at Fairfield and Geneva; in 1846, after studying abroad, he became the first professor of surgery at the University of Buffalo. Twelve years later, he became professor of surgery at the Long Island College Hospital in Brooklyn, New York, and in 1861, he was made professor of clinical and military surgery at the newly formed Bellevue Hospital Medical College.

Hamilton volunteered for army duty at the onset of the Civil War and was placed in charge of a field hospital for the 31st New York Volunteers at First Bull Run. He was rapidly promoted to brigade surgeon and then medical inspector, a rank just below that of Surgeon General. He

Frank Hastings Hamilton (1813–86).

served as a consultant and helped improve the quality of surgery at several major Union hospitals. He had written *Practical Treatise on Fractures and Dislocations* in 1860. Shortly after the war began, he published the first edition of his *Treatise on Military Surgery and Hygiene* (1862), which became the standard reference work for Union surgeons throughout the war. In September 1863, he resigned from the army and returned to Bellevue, where he became professor of surgery and surgical pathology. After the war, Hamilton helped with the writing and publication of the *Medical and Surgical History of the War of the Rebellion* and wrote numerous influential books on surgery. He consulted and helped treat the wounded President Garfield, but shortly after, he himself became too ill with tuberculosis to continue working.[1]

DR. OLIVER WENDELL HOLMES

Oliver Wendell Holmes (1809–94) was a noted physician, medical educator, humorist, poet, and author by the time of the Civil War. He was on the faculty of Harvard Medical School, where as Professor of Anatomy, he educated many prominent Civil War surgeons. He was widely known for his criticism of the excessive use of bleeding and administration of large doses of various toxic medications, such as mercury. He was also famous as a poet and raconteur and later for being the father of a Civil War officer who became a Supreme Court justice, Oliver Wendell Holmes, Jr. His son was wounded at Ball's Bluff in 1861 and at Antietam in 1862, but recovered and served through the rest of the war.

After graduating from Harvard College, Holmes earned his M.D. degree at Cambridge University in England in 1836. He then traveled in Europe and studied primarily in Paris, where one of his favorite teachers was Pierre Charles Alexandre Louis. Louis had introduced statistics to medicine and is considered one of the founders

Oliver Wendell Holmes. [From the collection of F. Terry Hambrecht, M.D.]

of modern clinical investigation. Holmes and other American students who had gone to Paris transmitted Louis' influence to generations of American medical students; Louis' methods are responsible for the organization and statistics used by the authors of the *Medical and Surgical History of the War of the Rebellion.*[2]

DR. ROBLEY DUNGLISON

Robley Dunglison was born in England. From 1815 to 1818, he studied medicine in London, Edinburgh, and Paris, and then passed the examinations of the Royal College of Surgeons and the Society of Apothecaries in London. As was common at the time, he earned his M.D. five years later (in 1823), from the University of Erlangen, Germany. After finding the general practice of medicine "distasteful," he decided to specialize in obstetrics and pediatrics.

Dr. Robley Dunglison.

When Thomas Jefferson was founding his new university in Charlottesville, Virginia, he commissioned Francis Walker Gilmer to find professors in England for the faculty. He specified that they be "characters of due degree of science, and of talents for instruction, and of correct habits and morals." In the fall of 1824, Gilmer offered the anatomy and medicine professorship to Dunglison. He signed the contract on September 28, 1824, hastily arranged to marry Miss Harriette Leadam, daughter of a fellow London physician, and set off for Virginia. They did not reach America until early February; the voyage was routinely made in four to five weeks, but it took them fourteen. (He never crossed the Atlantic again.) Dunglison began teaching the medical curriculum when the University of Virginia began classes on March 7, 1825. However, in 1833 he accepted a position as Chair of Materia Medica at the University of Maryland in Baltimore. Three years later, Dunglison accepted an offer from Jefferson Medical College in Philadelphia to serve as Chair of the Institutes of Medicine and Medical Jurisprudence. He spent the rest of his career at Jefferson, where many of the future Civil War surgeons of both sides were educated.

Dunglison was one of the most prolific medical writers of his time. He edited and translated European medical texts and contributed more than fifty original essays and books. He published nineteen editions of his dictionary of medical terminology, which was the prime reference for Civil War physicians. His textbook, *The Practice of Medicine,* also was widely used before the Civil War.

Dunglison also coedited the *American Dictionary for the Blind*—the first of its kind—and his *Human Physiology* (1832) earned him the reputation of "father of American physiology." *The American Journal of Medical Sciences* called Dunglison's book "the most complete and satisfactory system of physiology in the English language." The eighth and final edition appeared in 1856.[3,4]

Professor Dunglison's son, Thomas, served as an assistant surgeon in the Union Army. For part of the war he was stationed at the Lincoln Hospital in Washington.

MEDICAL SCHOOLS

The Jefferson Medical College was founded in 1824, primarily by faculty members of the University of Pennsylvania College of Medicine who wished to start an independent medical school. It was one of the most prominent medical schools of the country at the time of the Civil War, and many of the surgeons on both sides had trained there.

General George Brinton McClellan's father, Dr. George McClellan (1796–1847), was one of the founders of the Jefferson Medical College and was professor of anatomy and surgery there. Dr. Jonathan Letterman, who became Medical Director of the Army of the Potomac under General McClellan, graduated from the Jefferson Medical College in 1848.

The Medical College of Virginia's "Egyptian Building" housed the medical school in the years immediately preceding the Civil War. It was built in the style of Egyptian architecture that had become popular in Britain and the United States in the early decades of the nineteenth century, after Napoleon's campaign in Egypt in 1798 and the decipherment of hieroglyphics by Jean-François Champollion stimulated interest in ancient Egypt.

The Jefferson Medical College in Philadelphia.

The Egyptian Building of the Medical College of Virginia, Richmond.

In 1838 the Hampton-Sydney College established a medical department in Richmond, renamed the Medical College of Virginia in 1854. Many Confederate Civil War surgeons were educated there. Closed during the war, it reopened after the war, and Dr. Hunter Holmes. McGuire, who had been Stonewall Jackson's physician and the medical director of his corps, became a prominent member of the faculty there. A statue of Dr. McGuire was erected in Richmond late in the nineteenth century—the only statue of a Civil War surgeon to be installed until late in the twentieth century.[5]

OTHER PROMINENT MEDICAL EDUCATORS OF CIVIL WAR SURGEONS

Dr. Charles Smith, professor of surgery and author of key manual of military surgery used by Civil War surgeons.

Dr. Willard Parker (1800–84), prominent professor of medicine at the College of Physicians and Surgeons in New York, between 1839 and 1870.

ENDNOTES

1   Carlisle, R. J. *An Account of Bellevue Hospital, with a Catalogue of the Medical and Surgical Staff from 1736 to 1894*. New York: Society of the Alumni of Bellevue Hospital, 1893.

2   Hoyt, E. P. *The Improper Bostonian*. New York: Morrow, 1979.

3   Johnson, A., Malone, D., eds. *Dictionary of American Biography*, Vol. 8, New York: Scribner's, 1930, p. 185.

4   Garrison, F. H. *An Introduction to the History of Medicine*. Philadelphia: W. B. Saunders, 4th ed., 1929.

5   Schildt, John W (1986), *Hunter Holmes McGuire: Stonewall Jackson's Doctor*. Shippensburg, PA: White Mane Publishing, 2002.

3

NURSING

A T THE START OF THE WAR, there were few trained nurses in civilian life and none in the army. Family members did most civilian nursing, and any nursing that took place in the frontier army posts was done either by soldiers' wives or by other soldiers, usually patients themselves. Early in the Civil War, according to one contemporary description, nursing was done by "convalescent soldiers, wan, thin, weak, and requiring nursing themselves, and although they were kind to their comrades, they were wholly worthless as nurses."[1] If a soldier-nurse learned his tasks and began to do them well, he was usually declared healthy and transferred back to active duty.

Hospitals were still rudimentary at the time of the war, and nursing in civilian hospitals was little better than in military hospitals. Most patients were nursed at home; only people without adequate home facilities—such as the poor, the homeless, and out-of-town visitors—were admitted to a hospital. It was said of Bellevue Hospital, a leading hospital in New York before the war, that "at night no one attended the patients except the rats that roamed the floors."[2] Many hospitals of that era began as the infirmary for a poorhouse or jail, as did as Bellevue.[3] During an epidemic, the emergency need for nurses was met primarily by residents of the adjacent poorhouse or by prisoners detailed from the jail.

The initial lack of nursing care during the Civil War became critical soon after the war began, as epidemics, such as measles, spread rapidly among the recruits, augmented by large numbers of casualties from the early battles. Nursing was the most effective component of the treatment of serious illness in the middle of the nineteenth century. The development of nursing for Civil War soldiers played a major role in the evolution of the nursing profession in the United States.

NUNS

A t the time of the Civil War, the only training in nursing was that provided to some groups of Catholic sisters. In areas close to the fighting, such as in cities near northern Virginia after Bull Run, nuns of several orders left their ordinary functions and made themselves indispensable as hospital nurses. Subsequently, many surgeons in charge of hospitals specifically requested nursing help from a nearby order and the request was immediately granted. During the course of the war, at least twelve orders of nuns participated, including the Sisters of Charity (several branches), Sisters of Mercy, Sisters of St. Joseph, and Sisters of the Holy Cross.

Illustration showing a nun at a patient's bedside.

Nuns served on both sides and sometimes, as the fortunes of war changed on a battlefield, on both sides simultaneously.

The first nuns to enter the war as nurses were the Sisters of Charity of Emmittsburg, Maryland. They were asked for help by the Confederates in June 1861, even before First Bull Run. Shortly after that battle, Confederate General Joseph E. Johnston ordered the sick and wounded sent south, and the nuns went with them, ending up in Richmond. Later, Confederate Surgeon General Samuel Preston Moore "begged that the Sisters would take charge of the Stuart Hospital" in Richmond, which they did.[4]

The Sisters of Charity at Emmitsburg were repeatedly asked to provide nurses during the course of the war. In June 1862, Federal authorities telegraphed the Order asking if any Sisters could be detailed to work in nearby "Frederick City," Maryland. The following month, the Federal Surgeon General asked for 100 Sisters to be sent to White House, Virginia, to help during the chaos of the Peninsula campaign. General McClellan also requested help from the Order at Emmitsburg after Antietam. After Gettysburg, the Sisters attended the sick and wounded in the Catholic and Methodist churches in that town.

Both Presidents Lincoln and Davis complimented the nursing done by the nuns. Lincoln commended the nuns he saw in action, particularly on a visit to the Stanton Hospital. On one occasion, a letter from Lincoln warned a general that he would incur his displeasure if he interfered with the work of the Sisters of Charity. In an address to the sisters after the war, Jefferson Davis said: "I can never forget your kindness to the sick and wounded in our darkest days, and I know not how to testify my gratitude and respect for every member of your noble order."[5]

Mary Livermore, who established the Western Sanitary Commission and recorded her experiences in informative detail, summarized the feelings about the nuns: ". . . by their skill, quietness, gentleness, and tenderness, [they] were invaluable in the sick wards. Every patient gave hearty testimony to the kindness and skill of the 'Sisters.'"[6]

THE WOMEN WERE DETERMINED

In 1859, the last report of the British Commission on the Crimea War appeared, documenting the unnecessary suffering and enormous numbers of deaths from disease during that war (1854–56), as well as the impact of Florence Nightingale, who brought female nurses to the British base hospital in Turkey. These reports were widely read in the United States, and when the Civil War began, women worried that similar tragic developments would affect their sons and husbands who were volunteering for the armies. Determined to do something to prevent it, women's groups started to meet within days after the attack on Fort Sumter initiated the fighting on April 12 and 13.

Dorothea Dix, already well-known for her humanitarian efforts, observed that the army was not prepared to care for even the relatively few casualties that occurred on April 19 in the 6th Massachusetts Militia. The regiment had been attacked by a mob while en route to Washington, when it marched through Baltimore between train stations. Losing no time, she approached the War Department in Washington and offered to provide 100 trained nurses to keep the hospitals in hygienic condition, emphasizing the benefits that had been demonstrated earlier by Florence Nightingale. Initially ignored, she persisted, almost camping in the War Department and lobbying the Secretary of War and others whenever they appeared. Finally, she was made Superintendent of Female Nurses and given the authority to organize a woman's nursing corps. The army was to provide pay, transportation, and subsistence for the nurses. Dix then wrote to Dr. Elizabeth Blackwell in New York, the first woman to receive an M.D. degree in the United States. Dr. Blackwell had already invited socially prominent, concerned citizens to a meeting, from which arose the U.S. Sanitary Commission. Dix asked Blackwell to recruit and train the nurses, which she did.[7]

Dix insisted that her nurses be middle-aged, plain-looking women, dressed without ornamentation, who came from socially "respectable" families. These policies were necessary because of the low regard in which nurses were held at the time—many even being accused of prostitution—and she was determined to avoid such a stigma for her nurses. However, Dix's policies limited the number of nurses who could be accepted, despite the huge demand for more female nurses and the large number of volunteers. Dix's nurses were assigned almost exclusively

Unidentified nurse from Jefferson Hospital in Indiana.

Unidentified woman who served as a nurse at the Jefferson Hospital in Indiana.

to large general hospitals in major cities, especially in the Washington area. But these nurses represented only a small portion of the women who served as paid nurses, matrons, cooks, and laundresses in the Union Army. Dix's administrative methods were haphazard and her records were poor, seeming to list only about 3,200 women as serving in her corps of female army nurses over the course of the war. The army, however, paid at least 18,000 women for nursing services and roughly 2,000 more served as unpaid volunteers.

Newspaper reports and soldiers' letters describing the epidemics of disease in the camps on both sides in the late months of 1861 and early 1862 brought out hundreds of women volunteers from all social strata, largely independent of Dorothea Dix. Women simply appeared at military hospitals on both sides, despite the traditions that denied such opportunities to women. Prejudice against them and discourteous, even rude, treatment of them occurred in many instances, but the female volunteers quickly became so valuable that they were generally well accepted, and many earned official status. Some women were designated as "matrons," in charge of wards and of the soldier-nurses. Some worked in field hospitals in camps and near battlefields, sometimes in exposed areas, under fire, and they often helped to collect and care for wounded immediately after the fighting had stopped. Some women were actually enlisted by individual

Nursing scene at the military hospital in Georgetown, Maryland, occupying the facilities of the Union Hotel. Louisa Mae Alcott served as a nurse in this hospital late in 1862 and the first week of January, 1863, when typhoid fever abruptly ended her nursing career.

Unidentified woman from Jefferson Hospital.

Another unidentified nurse from Jefferson Hospital.

regiments and called "battle nurses," or even "daughters of the regiment." Others changed dressings, helped with surgical procedures, supervised other volunteer nurses, prepared food, especially extraordinary diets, and provided other comforts. (Occasionally, especially on the Southern side, they obtained much of the food.) Some women had greater responsibilities—Phoebe Yates Pember, for example, a matron at Chimborazo Hospital in Richmond, became an exceptional Confederate hospital administrator.

Dix usually insisted that her nurses be supervisors, with soldiers assigned to them to perform most of the tasks, a policy that often conflicted with the existing organization in hospitals and led to friction. Dix's attitude hampered the acceptance of her nurses. She was confrontational whenever she felt the doctors were not accepting her nurses properly or found them otherwise remiss. When anyone questioned her authority, Dix responded, "I am Dorothea L. Dix, Superintendent of Nurses, in the employ of the United States Government!"[8] Given their prewar social standing and contacts, Dix's nurses brought to bear a political influence that was often considerable, which did not increase their popularity with the medical staff. There was much less friction and more acceptance of the women as nurses in areas where Dix's role was negligible.

The friction that Dix created culminated in a directive from Surgeon General William Alexander Hammond on July 14, 1862. Although it repeated Dix's authorization to select and assign women nurses, it placed "control and direction" of all the nurses, women as well as men, under the "medical officer in charge." The order also specified one female nurse for every two male nurses. General Order No. 357, issued on October 27, 1863 (after Hammond had been removed), again emphasized that the female nurses were no longer under the exclusive supervision of Miss Dix and were not independent of the Medical Department staff; they were under the control of the senior medical officers in the hospital in which they served. This order meant they could be assigned other duties or dismissed for incompetence or disobedience. The order also contained economy measures, specifying no more than one nurse per thirty beds and reducing the pay of nurses from $20.50 a month to $13, plus a $3 allowance for clothing. Dix was devastated, and her influence waned as the war went on.

In hotels that were taken over for use as hospitals, finding quarters for female nurses was not a major problem because individual rooms could be assigned to them. In other institutions, there was a lot of friction between physicians—who saw no need for females in the busy, smelly, crowded hospital facilities—and the women, especially Dix's women. Curtains were hung to isolate specific areas, and, as the women showed their usefulness, better and better facilities were arranged. The problem was solved by an order from the Secretary of War requiring that in newly constructed hospitals, a separate building be erected and assigned to the female nursing staff. In the chapter on hospitals in the *Medical and Surgical History*, ground plans for a number of hospitals are shown, with the separate building for women designated in the legend. For example, see the plans and description of the Armory Square Hospital in Washington, D.C. and the DeCamp General Hospital in New Rochelle, New York.

Clara Barton served as a nurse in the field, independent of Dorothea Dix. Originally from Massachusetts, she was a clerk in the patent office in Washington when the war began. Learning of the injuries to the 6th Massachusetts, on April 19, she sought and finally found that, after they arrived in Washington, the wounded were housed in the Capitol's rotunda. Arriving there, she found that the men needed food and other supplies and that some were not receiving necessary medical and nursing care. Using her own resources, she began to dress wounds as well as she could and to provide food and other necessities. A newspaperman from Boston, who had

Midnight on the battlefield. (From the collection of F. Terry Hambrecht, M.D.) This painting documents an episode at Fort Donelson, when Mary Bickerdyke went out onto the battlefield after dark, checking bodies, searching for wounded men who were still alive and had not been brought in.

come to see his hometown troops, reported on Barton's work, and the resulting publicity produced a flood of contributions and gifts. With these funds, as well as the political help necessary to obtain battlefield passes (Senator Henry Wilson from Massachusetts was a close friend of Barton's), she was able to continue working on her own, purchasing supplies, hiring wagons and drivers, and moving with the army when fighting broke out. She worked in the field and later in general hospitals in several areas, serving for the entire war. She was especially useful at Hilton Head and in treating troops engaged in the attacks on Fort Wagner, near Charleston.

Many of the nurses suffered terrible consequences in the course of "doing their duty." An unrecorded number suffered severe illness; several died of typhoid fever and other diseases acquired while caring for sick soldiers. Louisa Mae Alcott, one of Miss Dix's troops, worked for a few months at the Union Hotel, which was converted to a military hospital in Georgetown. She developed typhoid fever, suffered severe toxicity in the mercury she was given as treatment, and almost died before her father arrived and took her home. Despite Alcott's brief tenure, the description of her experiences as "Nurse Periwinkle" in her *Hospital Sketches* is charming and informative.[9]

One of the most notable women who served on the Union side was Mary Ann Bickerdyke. Known as "Mother Bickerdyke" to the men and to posterity, she was so effective that she received special protection and support from Generals Ulysses S. Grant and William Tecumseh Sherman. Bickerdyke followed the latter's army until he began his March to the Sea in late 1864. A housekeeper for a wealthy Chicago family, her lowly social status would have made her unacceptable to Dorothea Dix. Mrs. Bickerdyke appeared at the army base in Cairo, Illinois, delivering supplies. When she saw the dire need for her services, she simply stayed and went to work. She procured equipment and supplies through the Northwestern Branch of the Sanitary Commission and established diet kitchens and laundries. She acquired a veritable army of freed or runaway slaves, known as "contrabands," who worked effectively under her direction in these facilities; there were so many under her command, she was sometimes called "General Bickerdyke."[10] Famous for her common sense, energy, and unswerving devotion to her "boys," she received full support from Generals Grant and Sherman to cut through army red tape.

Bickerdyke served with the Western Union Army throughout the war, including in the Vicksburg and Atlanta campaigns. Her affection for her "boys" was returned; they usually called her "Mother." At the end of the war, they insisted she accompany them during the army's "Grand Review" on May 23, 1865, riding in an ambulance wagon down Washington's "Chiefest Avenue."

Photo of Winnie Davis, daughter of the confederate President, Jefferson Davis, used as an advertisement for an "iron tonic." (From the collection of F. Terry Hambrecht, M.D.)

DR. MARY EDWARDS WALKER (1832–1919)

Although some details of the career of Dr. Walker are vague, the fact that she was a woman doctor who served the Union cause in heroic fashion is not in doubt. She was born in Oswego, New York, and graduated from Syracuse Medical College during the 1840s or 1850s. She was struggling to establish a medical practice in Cincinnati and, when the Civil War began, she worked as a nurse in the Union Army for three years. An Ohio regiment finally hired her in 1864 as a contract physician. Allowed to pass back and forth through the Union and Confederate lines, Walker was able to function as a spy and report on her observations. In October 1864, she received a formal army commission as an Assistant Surgeon and functioned in that official capacity until the war ended. She was captured while treating a Confederate soldier on a battlefield and spent four months in a Confederate prison.

Postwar image of Dr. Mary Walker, in male attire. Photo by George Prince, Washington, D.C. (From the collection of F. Terry Hambrecht, M.D.)

While in the army, Dr. Walker wore a military uniform, as shown on the facing page, and wore her hair long so people would know she was a woman. After the war, she continued to wear male attire and became active in women's rights movements. In 1897, she tried to establish a colony for women only, calling it "Adamless Eden." Her militancy apparently caused most people, including her family, to shun her and she died poor and alone in the city of her birth.

Her dangerous exploits during the Civil War led to the award of a Medal of Honor. However, after the criteria for awarding such medals were reconsidered, the Board of Medals officially revoked the medal and asked her to return it. She is reported to have said, "They can have it over my dead body." She died the next day, February 21, 1919. In 1977, the award was officially reinstated.[11]

Dr. Mary Edwards Walker, Acting Assistant Surgeon and Medal of Honor recipient.

ENDNOTES

1   Livermore, M., *My Story of the War: A Woman's Narrative of Four Year's Personal Experience as a Nurse in the Union Army.* Hartford, Conn.: A. D. Worthington & Co., 1892, p. 203.

2   Nutting, M. E., Dock, L.L., *A History of Nursing: The Evolution of Nursing from the Earliest Times to the Foundation of the First English and American Training Schools for Nurses.* New York: Putnam, 1907.

3   Carlisle, R. J., ed. *An Account of Bellevue Hospital.* New York: Society of the Alumni of Bellevue Hospital, 1893 (repub. 1986), p. 35.

4   Candido, J. H., Sisters and nuns who were nurses during the Civil War. *Blue and Gray Magazine,* 1993; vol. x: pp. 11–30.

5   Barton, G., *Angels of the Battlefield: A History of the Labors of the Catholic Sisterhoods during the Late Civil War.* Philadelphia: Catholic Arts Publishing Co., 1897, pp. 169, 174.

6   Livermore, *My Story of the War,* p. 218.

7   Greenbie, M. B., *Lincoln's Daughters of Mercy,* G. P. Putnam's Sons, 1944, p. 61.

8   Oates, S. B., *A Woman of Valor: Clara Barton and the Civil War.* New York: MacMillan, 1994, p. 23.

9   Alcott, L. M., *Hospital Sketches.* (Bessie Z. Jones, ed.) Cambridge, Mass: Harvard Univ. Press, 1960.

10 Greenbie, *Lincoln's Daughters of Mercy,* p. 191.

11 Faust, P. L., ed. *Historical Times Encyclopedia of the Civil War.* New York: Harper & Row, 1986, p. 798.

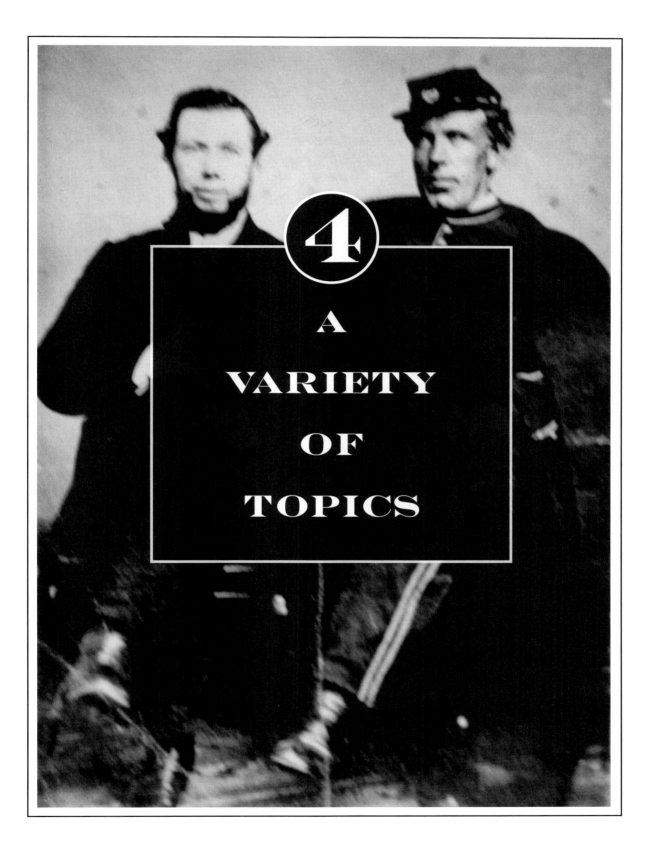

4

A
VARIETY
OF
TOPICS

THE U.S. SANITARY COMMISSION

The American public knew a great deal about Florence Nightingale and her team of thirty-eight nurses, who were sent to British military hospitals in Turkey during the Crimean War by the British Sanitary Commission, a quasigovernmental organization. They cared for soldiers, improved cleanliness, and established other sanitary measures, decreasing the monthly death rate dramatically. Despite general belief that the Civil War would be brief, at the outset of the fighting, groups of American civilians gathered, concerned that the pre-Nightingale medical catastrophes of the Crimean War would be repeated here.

Soldiers' Aid Societies, formed by groups of Union women, began to meet as early as April 15, 1861, one day after Major Robert Anderson surrendered Fort Sumter. Dr. Elizabeth Blackwell, the first woman physician in the United States, organized a meeting of socially prominent New York women at the Cooper Institute on April 29. They decided to form the Women's Central Association of Relief of New York City.

U.S. Sanitary Commission facility at Gettysburg operating in a small private home called the "Widow Listen House." It served primarily as a distribution center. Wounded soldiers were brought here from the battlefield and then sent to larger field hospitals or to Camp Letterman, the general hospital that stayed in operation until late November, 1863.

In May 1861, the Rev. Dr. Henry Whitney Bellows, pastor of All Souls Unitarian Church in New York City, and Dr. Elisha Harris, a prominent New York physician, following the lead of Blackwell and the other women, formed the U.S. Sanitary Commission. The Women's Central Association of Relief of New York City became a component of the larger organization. The U.S. Sanitary Commission remained an independent civilian organization. The Women's Central Association sponsored Dorothea Dix, who became the supervisor of female nurses for the Union Army, and then established a training program for army nurses planning to serve with Miss Dix.

U.S. Sanitary Commission facility set up after the Battle of Gettysburg.

Representatives of the U.S. Sanitary Commission traveled to Washington on May 16, 1861, to meet the acting surgeon general of the army, Colonel Robert C. Wood, who had just assumed that position following the death of Surgeon General Thomas Lawson, a veteran of the War of 1812 who had become surgeon general when John Quincy Adams was president. Wood was polite during the meeting but noncommittal, clearly just humoring them in hopes they would go away.[1] After damning public criticism resulting from the chaos in caring for the wounded at Bull Run, the newly appointed surgeon general, Clement Finley, yielded to pressure and allowed the U.S. Sanitary Commission a role. However, he limited the Commission to assisting in the care of the volunteer army, not the regular army troops. That suited the Commission because the regular army was rapidly becoming a tiny percentage of the Union's total force.[2] The Commission established its offices in the Treasury building on September 16, 1861.

Rev. Gordon Winslow of the U.S. Sanitary Commission, who died during the war.

The U.S. Sanitary Commission inspected army camps, evaluating such health practices as sanitation, water supply, and diet of the troops. It also evaluated the surgeons, most of whom were appointed by state governors without any consideration of ability. The Commission made strong recommendations about cleaning up the camps and instituting standard sanitary practices, and recommended removal of the surgeons whom it found to be "negligent and inert."[3] The Commission established field offices in army camps and then near battlefields, bringing supplies and supplementary food to the soldiers and much needed supplies after a battle. During the Peninsula campaign of 1862, when evacuation of the wounded became chaotic, the U.S. Sanitary Commission was especially useful in the removal of wounded and sick soldiers; ships were obtained and staffed as floating hospitals. Although the ships lacked proper facilities and the absence of military discipline and organization led to considerable confusion during evacuation of the wounded, the value of hospital ships became clear. The Commission donated its hospital boats to the army, which staffed and ran them for the remainder of the war. Additional boats were purchased by the army and refitted to serve as hospital ships; many became famous during the war for the improvements they brought in the evacuation and care of the wounded in the Chesapeake Bay and Potomac River areas, and along the Mississippi and other western rivers, although these ships were not generally placed under the control of the Medical Department until early 1865.[4]

As the incompetence of the army's medical leadership became glaringly apparent, pressure from the U.S. Sanitary Commis-

Rev. Winslow in front of a U.S. Sanitary Commission tent in the field at Gettysburg.

Michigan Sanitary Commission facility in the field.

Sanitary Commission field headquarters at an unspecified location.

sion and the press forced Secretary of War Edwin Stanton to remove the incompetent Surgeon General Clement Finley. Ignoring the seniority system, Stanton appointed the relatively junior army physician recommended by the Commission, William Hammond, on April 25, 1862 (see photo and brief biography in Chapter 6 on CDVs of Union physicians.) The Commission fought to have an ambulance corps established. Later, after the Union Medical Department had been reorganized and an ambulance corps created, civilian help was not so sorely needed and the Commission contributed to the care of the soldiers in other ways.

The Commission was particularly valuable on the spot with badly needed medical supplies immediately after the Battle of Gettysburg, when the army's stores had arrived late following the precipitous move into Pennsylvania in pursuit of Lee's army. During the Overland Campaign, after the battles of May and June, 1864, at the Wilderness, Spottsylvania, and Cold Harbor, when the army Medical Department was again overwhelmed with casualties, the Sanitary Commission provided a great deal of help, especially in the town of Fredericksburg.

As documented elsewhere, the Commission provided many services to soldiers. It operated "soldiers' rest homes," which afforded troops a place to stay and be well fed while en route home on furlough or after discharge. It kept a registry of hospitalized soldiers so that family members hoping to visit could learn where their loved ones were being cared for. The Commission published numerous "bulletins" documenting the experience of surgeons in care of wounds and illness, with advice based on those experiences. Its articles were especially helpful in promoting bromine—effective in the treatment of hospital gangrene—and making recommendations for prevention of scurvy and treatment of chronic diarrhea.

To support its activities, one of the fund-raising methods of the U.S. Sanitary Commission was the organization of great fund-raising "fairs," which featured exhibits of various kinds, balls, and similar activities. These fairs were held in most large cities of the North and in some foreign countries, including England (in London). During the course of the war, the Commission raised a total of $1.2 million.

A separate but related Western Sanitary Commission raised its own money, held large "sanitary fairs," and provided similar services for the western Union armies. One of its main accomplishments was to support Mary Bickerdyke (discussed in Chapter 3, Nursing).

THE U.S. CHRISTIAN COMMISSION

The Christian Commission was organized by the Young Men's Christian Association in New York City on November 14, 1861. The main organizer, Vincent Colyer, later became president of the YMCA. During the Civil War, the Christian Commission provided many services similar to those furnished by the U.S. Sanitary Commission, including supplying food and medical supplies to soldiers and visiting men in hospitals. Women in the organization performed nursing services. Initially, the Christian Commission worked in conjunction with the U.S. Sanitary Commission, but, later, strained relationships developed.

Field headquarters of the U. S. Christian Commission at an unspecified location.

The Christian Commission felt a duty to provide moral and spiritual as well as physical aid. It distributed Bibles along with food, medical supplies, and material to write letters home. It also strenuously fought the consumption of alcohol by the troops. Some critics contended that the Christian Commission's interest in distributing Bibles and religion took too much precedence over its other activities. The Commission raised and spent more than six million dollars to support its work in the war. It went out of existence February 11, 1866.[5]

DENTISTRY

Dentistry was still in an early phase of its development at the time of the Civil War. The first American dental school, the Baltimore College of Dentistry, opened in 1840 with five students; by 1860, there were only about 400 graduates of the three dental schools then existing in the United States. However, there were about 5,500 dental practitioners, most trained by apprenticeships. The Southern states had about 1,000 dentists at the start of the war, but no dental schools.[6]

A plan to institute a Dental Corps in the U.S. Army in the 1850s, supported by Jefferson Davis, then Secretary of War, was endorsed by Thomas Lawson, then Surgeon General, but it was never approved by Congress. When a similar plan was proposed after the Civil War began, the War Department opposed the idea. Therefore, regimental surgeons, who could do little but pull teeth and lance gum boils, provided what dental services were available to the troops. Tooth extractions were often incomplete, leaving the roots behind to cause problems later. Union soldiers often had to consult civilian dentists when they needed care, paying for the services from their own pockets. For example, when Sherman's troops reached Savannah, his men besieged dental offices. A local dentist estimated that "the emergency need alone would have required 100 dentists to work six months on these troops."[7] (One wonders whether the luxurious feasting by Sherman's men during the March to the Sea might have precipitated these dental problems.)

As the physical examinations for Union recruits improved, extensive cavities, numerous missing teeth, and bad periodontal disease were listed as causes for rejection. The records, however, show relatively few actual rejections for these reasons. The regulations established to guide physicians examining potential recruits or draftees considered as a handicap only the absence of the four front incisors, since, in order to load their guns, soldiers had to tear open paper cartridges with those teeth. Only 2.4 percent of the men examined were excused from

Union military service for lack of teeth. The records of men excused from service because of the absence of the four front teeth were marked "4F" to indicate the nature of this disability. Later, the abbreviation came to refer to any medical reason for draft deferral.

CONFEDERATE ARMY DENTISTRY

Because of a shortage of manpower, the Confederates could not afford to reject men with dental problems. At the start of the war, Surgeon General Moore calculated that, by drafting dentists into the regular army, many men who might have been rejected or dismissed from military service could instead be treated and retained. He arranged for dentists to be commissioned as captains or majors.

Dentists were assigned primarily to the larger military hospitals; every soldier admitted to these hospitals was required to have a dental exam. Because dentists usually lived some distance from the hospital, they were provided with an ambulance wagon for transportation, but they had to provide their own instruments. As the war progressed, medical and dental supplies became increasingly difficult to obtain because the Federal government declared all medical and surgical equipment and supplies contraband of war.

The workload for hospital dentists was prodigious. Each day they performed twenty to thirty fillings and fifteen to twenty extractions, and they removed immense amounts of tartar.[8] However, as in the Union Army, Confederate soldiers who needed artificial teeth had to go to a civilian dentist at their own expense. Gold had been a favorite material for denture bases, but by the time of the Civil War, the civilian dentists were using vulcanite. (Vulcanite was India rubber, heated with sulfur to harden it. An American inventor, Charles Goodyear, invented the process in 1839.)

Dentists inserted fillings using first a hand-rotated drill bit and then hand excavators to remove carious material and undercut the margins so that the filling would be retained. They then inserted the filling material and filed or burnished it smooth. If the pulp was exposed, creosotum was often inserted into the pulp chamber, followed by gold foil for small fillings; however, because it was cheaper, they used tin foil for larger ones. An amalgam of silver, tin, and mercury also was widely used, especially when it was difficult to insert gold. Archeological explorations have permitted analyses of the tooth fillings of several Confederate soldiers. Most were filled with gold foil; however, one was filled with thorium. (Thorium was discovered in 1828, but it was not known to be radioactive until 1898. Commercially available by the middle of the century, it is a relatively abundant mineral and can be shaped fairly easily.) The dentists probably thought it was tin; of course, they knew nothing about radioactivity. One tooth even had a filling consisting of lead and shotgun pellets![9]

Dentists on both sides did more complicated oral surgery when injuries caused jaw fractures. Some complex devices to immobilize the mandible were invented, including one used on Secretary of State William Henry Seward when he had a bad carriage accident. The complicated external apparatus is thought to have saved his life when an assassin tried to stab him in the neck on the night President Lincoln was shot.

Civilian contract dentist posed with a commanding officer (not identified). Civilian dentists, such as the one shown in this photograph, were employed by the Union Army to care for the dental problems of soldiers and, in some instances, cared for prisoners of war.

EMBALMING

Routine embalming was common by the time of the Civil War, at least for wealthy people or politically important figures. When the war started, embalmers flocked to the battlefields seeking business. Over the course of the war, demand for embalming grew with the number of casualties. The technique of injecting the body with preservatives through a femoral artery was quite effective, and coffins containing embalmed remains were commonplace on trains and ships heading to the North. The usual charge for embalming and shipping a body home was about fifty dollars for an officer and twenty-five dollars for an enlisted man, but by late in the war, eighty dollars and thirty dollars, respectively, were more common charges.[10]

Because Civil War soldiers wore no name tags, identification of the corpses was often very difficult; as a result, about half of the graves in Civil War battlefields are marked "unknown." Soldiers who died in a hospital were much more likely to be identified, and their bodies were also more likely to be embalmed and shipped home.

A physician named C. H. Cleveland published a *Physician's Pocket Memorandum* in 1869 that included a description of the embalming techniques used during the war. According to the pamphlet:

Facility set up by embalming surgeon Bunnell.

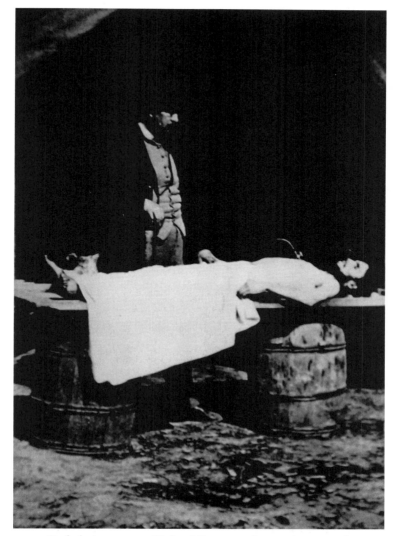

Embalming surgeon Richard Burr, posed preparing to work.

A strong solution of zinc chloride—1/2 ounce of the salt to a quart of alcohol and water—may be employed directly into the artery to prevent decomposition. Creosote (carbolic acid) may be used as an anti-putrefactive, but its odor is objectionable. . . . With a common pewter syringe, it may be thrown into the arterial system, the nozzle of the instrument being introduced into a slit made in the femoral artery.

It is customary to transport bodies in metallic burial cases, or heavy wooden boxes lined with zinc plates.[11]

PURVEYORS

Tent of W.G. Johnson, Purveyor, 2nd Division, 9th Corps, Army of the Potomac. No. 2448, negative by Brady & Co., Washington, D.C. Published by E. & H. T. Anthony & Co., N.Y. (From the collection of F. Terry Hambrecht, M.D.)

Purveyors were responsible for obtaining supplies for the Army, including drugs, food, and clothing. Purveyors were located in major cities throughout the country.

ENDNOTES

1   Maxwell, *Lincoln's Fifth Wheel: The Political History of the United States Sanitary Commission*. New York: Longman Green, 1956, pp. 6, 7.

2   Ibid.,

3   Wiley, B. I., *The Life of Billy Yank*. Baton Rouge: Louisiana State Univ. Press, 1952, p. 130. Quoting U.S. Sanitary Commission Documents Nos. 40, 33.

4   Gillette, M., *The Army Medical Department, 1818–1865*, Washington, DC: Center of Military History, U.S. Army, 1987, p. 295.

5   Faust, P. L., ed. *Historical Times Encyclopedia of the Civil War*. New York: Harper & Row, 1986, p. 140.

6   Tebo, H. G., Oral Surgery in the Confederate Army. *Bulletin of the History of Dentistry*. 1976; 24:28

7   Dammann, G., Dental Care during the Civil War. *Illinois Dental Journal*. 1984; 53:12.

8   Burton, W. L., Dental Surgery as Applied in the Armies of the Late Confederate States. *American Journal of Dental Science*. 1867;1:185.

9   Glenner, R. A., and P. Willey. Dental Filling Materials in the Confederacy. *Journal of the History of Dentistry*. 1998; 46:71.

10 Habenstein, R. W., *The History of American Funeral Directing*. 2nd rev. ed. Milwaukee: National Funeral Directors Assoc., 1981, p. 209.

11 Dammann, G., *A Pictorial Encyclopedia of Civil War Medical Instruments and Equipment*. Missoula: Pictorial Histories Publishing Co., 1983.

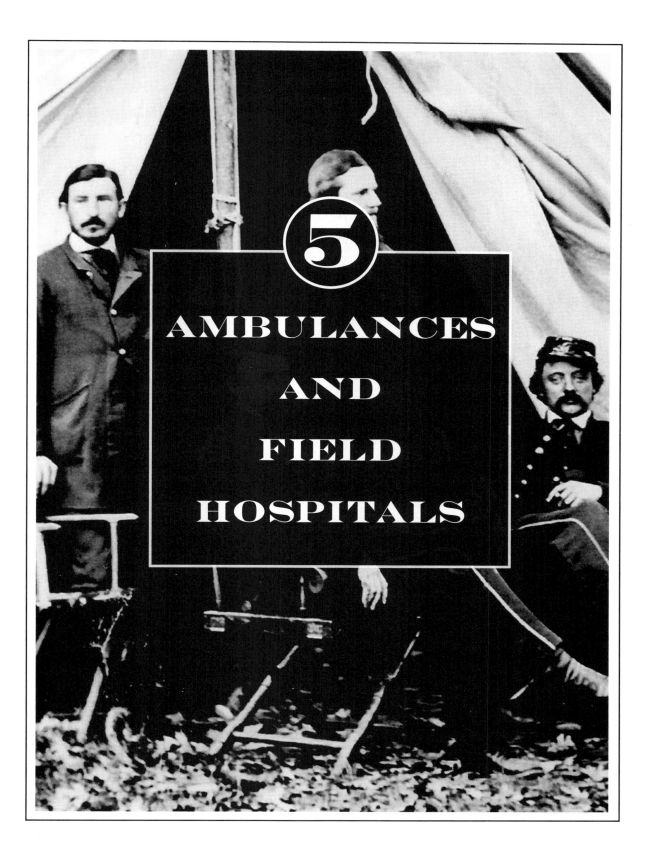

5

AMBULANCES AND FIELD HOSPITALS

THE ORGANIZATION OF AN AMBULANCE SERVICE and field hospital system were innovations in military medicine during the Civil War that have received consistent praise, nationally and internationally. Such a military medical transport system was unprecedented—no army had organized as efficient an ambulance service or delivered better medical care up to that time—and the arrangements, called "the American system," were widely copied in Europe. It took ten days or more to collect all of the wounded in earlier European wars, especially at the notable Battle of Solferino near Milan in 1859 (where the suffering of the wounded led to the creation of the International Red Cross*); it took a similar period to collect the wounded at both Battles of Bull Run. However, a new system was initiated in the Army of the Potomac by Dr. Jonathan Letterman during the summer of 1862, and the system was first put into almost full operation at the Battle of Antietam in September. At the Battle of Gettysburg in July 1863, the day after the battle ended, "not one wounded man of the great number who had fallen was left on the ground."[1]

THE AMBULANCE SYSTEM

Until two years before the start of the war, the U.S. Army had no vehicles specifically designed to be ambulances and no soldiers trained or even designated to remove the wounded from the field. The vehicles in use when the war began were mostly two-wheeled wagons, pulled by one or two horses or mules. Called "gutbusters" by the soldiers, they gave harsh, jolting rides and were easily upset, dumping occupants onto the ground and seriously aggravating their injuries. They were also too small, containing at most three men, and too light and frail in construction, breaking down quickly on the muddy, rutted roads of the era.

The dismal U.S. road system of the time, particularly in the South, added to the excruciating nature of the ambulance rides. Some of the main "turnpikes" had a macadam surface, made up of compacted layers of broken stone, which was considered good for wagons but bad for shoes. Most other roads had dirt surfaces and were rough, rutted, and almost impassable in wet weather. To establish a firm surface above the mud, logs were cut and spread crosswise,

---

*A witness to the disastrous plight of the wounded at that battle, Henri Dunant, called a Convention to create an organization "for the Amelioration of the Condition of the Wounded Soldiers of Armies in the Field." The convention met in Geneva in 1864 and the organization became the International Red Cross

Surg. Jonathan Letterman served as Medical Director of the Army of the Potomac between July 1, 1862 and the end of 1863. On the left, Dr. Letterman (seated at center) is seen with his staff.

a process called "corduroying." This decreased the likelihood of wagons getting mired in mud, but the resulting jolting ride was a torment to wounded men, especially those who had broken bones or who had freshly amputated arms or legs.

Compounding the problem, the ambulances were under the Quartermaster Department of each army corps, and supply needs often took priority for their use. Ambulances also could be commandeered for a variety of purposes, including the transport of officers' baggage, and thus were often unavailable to transport the wounded or sick when needed.

When Dr. Jonathan Letterman took over as Medical Director of the Army of the Potomac from Charles S. Tripler, early in July 1862, the major battles near Richmond on the peninsula had just ended. At that point, fully one-quarter of the Army of the Potomac—20,000 sick and wounded—were in hospitals at Harrison's Landing, the army's base on the James River where the guns of the fleet helped protect them. Tripler had a plan for a separate ambulance service under the Medical Department, but he was stymied by army regulations. Letterman persuaded General McClellan to ignore the regulations and form an ambulance corps. McClellan, an able administrator even if a poor field commander, ordered Letterman's plan implemented in the Army of the Potomac on August 2. His order directed that the Ambulance Corps be placed under the Medical Department—with its own animals, vehicles, and personnel—and that the

Demonstration of an unusual type of litter for carrying wounded suspended from a single pole. The soldier in front may be a hospital steward judging from his uniform.

Corps be used for sick and wounded men and "nothing else."[2] The order also required that trained personnel be designated as stretcher bearers and teamsters.

Before the reorganization of the field hospital and ambulance systems, wounded soldiers were a major hindrance to the effectiveness of a fighting force during a battle. Other soldiers often abandoned their positions in the battle line to help carry an injured buddy to whatever medical care was available, often a considerable distance away, thus depleting the firing line by two to four additional soldiers. One surgeon recorded that, at first, regimental band members transported the most severely wounded men, but soon there were no band members left.[3] Moreover, because of the time spent seeking the field station, these transporters rarely returned to the line before the action ended. On the field, improvised litters were made from anything available, such as doors, window shutters, ladders, gates removed from fences, poles through the sleeves of coats, blankets lashed to poles, and four-armed "chair seats." Occasionally they used chair-like contrivances strapped to a mule's back, called horse litters or *cacolets* (the French name). *Cacolets* had been used in the Crimean War and in Algeria by the French, but they were cumbersome and required trained animals; they were described by Surgeon John Brinton as

Union Army ambulance park; vehicles and staff ready to go into action.

Ambulance drill, 114th Pennsylvania Volunteers. Note the sergeant directing the action, the fake "casualties" waiting to be picked up, and the orderly way men on stretchers were being placed into the ambulance. These training drills resulted in efficient, dependable action during battles and made the evacuation of wounded much better than it had been early in the war.

Lieutenant William Burgess, commander of the ambulance unit of the First Brigade of the 6th Pennsylvania Reserves. When the ambulances were put under the control of the Medical Department, officers were placed in charge of ambulance units and brought discipline and dependability to the previously unorganized, chaotic system.

"only a troublesome and barbarous encumbrance, cruel alike to the wounded and the pack-animals." *Cacolets* were rarely used after 1862.

The army's fighting power was significantly strengthened when specific men were designated as stretcher bearers, ambulances with dependable drivers were stationed nearby, and soldiers no longer left the line to carry a wounded comrade.

Captain G. Tousley of the 84th Illinois, Commander of the Ambulances of the 4th Army Corps. Tousley was specifically commended for the efficiency of his ambulance system by the commander of the 4th Corps, Major General U. S. Stanley, after action in Northern Alabama and middle-Tennessee, in December 1864 and January 1865.[19] He was also commended by Brig. Gen's Thomas Wood who commanded the 4th Corps at an earlier point in the same campaign:. "Surg. Heard, medical director, Surg. Brumley, medical inspector, and Captain Tousley, chief of ambulances, performed their duties most satisfactorily. Ample preparation had been made in advance for the wounded, and humane and efficient care was promptly rendered them."[20]

Badge of the Ambulance Corps, Confederate States Army. ID badge and image of Private Falling, U.S. Army Ambulance Corps.

Thanks to McClellan's decision to implement Letterman's plan, the Army of the Potomac developed an effective ambulance system well before the western Federal Armies. Surgeon General Hammond proposed this new ambulance system for the entire Federal Army. In a letter to Secretary of War Stanton, on September 7, 1862, he lamented "the scarcity of ambulances, the want of organization, the drunkenness and incompetency of the drivers, [and] the total absence of ambulance attendants. . . ."[4] Although Hammond's request was rejected by both General-in-Chief Henry W. Halleck and Secretary of War Stanton, General Grant implemented a similar system in the western armies on March 30, 1863, ignoring the War Department's opposition.[5] The new structure of the ambulance service became official army policy when Congress finally passed a reorganization bill on March 11, 1864. By then, however, it was already in effect in most of the Union Army.

The Confederate ambulance system was greatly improved during the war, largely resulting from the suggestions of Dr. Hunter Holmes McGuire, who had served as medical director of Stonewall Jackson's Corps.[6] The Confederates adopted a system resembling that of the Union armies; although the ambulances remained technically under the Quartermaster, usually the medical directors and chief surgeons had adequate control over them.[7]

Union Army boards met repeatedly to improve ambulance design during the course of the war, and four-wheeled vehicles with springs came into general use.[8] Although the ride was never pleasant—and nursing care was negligible during transport—the new evacuation system helped minimize the amount of time wounded soldiers spent in the ambulance wagons. A key component of this new system was the establishment of field hospitals to which men could be taken quickly by trained personnel and given immediate care, with the ambulances rapidly available for new patients.

FIELD HOSPITALS

At the beginning of the war, regimental hospitals were established in campsites and, during battles, near the scene of action of individual regiments. Early in the war, wounded were turned away from regimental field hospitals if they were from the wrong regiment—because each regiment had only one surgeon and one assistant surgeon, regiments were often overwhelmed with their own casualties (or expected to be). Stretcher bearers had to search for the appropriate regimental field hospital in the confusion and smoke of a battle, leading to delayed treatment.

When Jonathan Letterman took over as Medical Director of the Army of the Potomac, he reorganized the field medical service. By late in 1862, regimental hospitals were abolished, and the practice of turning away men from the wrong unit ceased. Under Letterman's direction, the division hospital became the primary field unit. Each typically had a surgeon-in-chief, three operating surgeons, nine assistant surgeons, a medical officer who was responsible for securing food and shelter, and numerous assigned enlisted soldiers who functioned as nurses or stewards. The surgeon-in-chief, one of the most experienced surgeons, was usually a member of the operating team.[11] There were also some brigade-level hospitals, but most of the surgery done in the immediate care of the wounded was performed in divisional field hospitals. Hospital tents and medical supplies for field hospitals were issued on a brigade or divisional basis, and the availability of facilities and the organization of surgical care for the wounded remained a standard for both European and American armies through World War II.

Civil War surgeons knew that if amputation (by far the most common form of surgery done) was necessary, it had to be done within about forty-eight hours, and the sooner the procedure was performed, the better the likely outcome. They realized that once "tumefaction" had developed, it would be too dangerous to operate. Tumefaction was the term used for the firm swelling that results from inflammation; Civil War surgeons knew its prognostic significance, understanding from experience that surgical intervention usually led to "blood poisoning," or "pyemia," with a fatal outcome. Decades later, it was realized that the inflammation meant the presence of bacterial infection and that manipulating or cutting into an infected area caused the infection to spread.

Mrs. Spinners' house, used as a hospital on July 21, 1861, during the Battle of Bull Run. A large number of wounded Federal troops, and a member of congress, the Hon. A. Ely, were captured when a force of Confederate cavalry raided the house. Subsequently, Confederate wounded were treated there.

Early in the war, regimental surgeons usually worked alone, with the regimental assistant surgeon assigned to man a field aid station nearer to the battlefield. He would pick a spot sheltered from small arms fire if possible, but usually still subject to artillery fire. In these field aid stations, the assistant surgeon administered emergency care, including application of pressure or tourniquets to stop bleeding, immobilization of a wounded extremity with splints, and improvising some type of wound dressing; opiates were administered freely and triage decisions were made. Men who were not believed to be mortally wounded were evacuated first, usually in an ambulance, back to a field hospital that had been set up—hopefully out of artillery range—in an available building or in tents. At these field hospitals, supervising surgeons made decisions, and operating surgeons performed any operations deemed necessary.

Mobile field hospitals, which could go "wherever the needs of battle demanded and wheeled vehicles could penetrate," were promptly adopted by all Civil War armies and by the military of other countries. Sick or wounded men needing more extensive or prolonged care were transferred from field hospitals to larger fixed hospitals in the rear as soon as they could be moved.

These field hospitals, which were set up where needed and moved as necessary, evolved into the mobile hospitals employed by later U.S. armies during fast-moving army operations, such as the dash across France by General George Patton's Third Army and the Mobile Army Surgical Hospitals (M.A.S.H.) units of the Korean War, but the horse-drawn ambulances were replaced by motorized vehicles or helicopters. The same system was used in Vietnam, and in recent wars in the Persian Gulf area.

One regimental surgeon described a Civil War field hospital as follows:

When a battle was expected, [a decision regarding] the general location of the hospital was made. . . . It was intended to be in the rear of the ground on which the division was expected to fight, and beyond the enemy's artillery fire, one and a half or two miles in the rear of our line of battle; if possible a good supply of water must be at hand. All the tents were set up, dressings, instruments, and tables for dressing and operating prepared, and everything made ready for our work.

Three assistant surgeons and one surgeon were detailed to follow each brigade. They established a temporary depôt just out of reach of the enemy's musketry fire.

Amputation scene at field hospital at Fortress Monroe. In view of the exposure time necessary to take photographs during the Civil War, this scene was probably posed. Wounded from the Peninsula Campaign were evacuated to Fortress Monroe for care, before being sent north using improvised hospital boats.

Surgeon examining soldier's leg at improvised field hospital at Savage Station during the Seven Days Battles near Richmond in June 1862. The locale was at a station on the railroad line that was used to transport the wounded to Harrison's Landing where boats were available to take them north.

Here the ambulances stopped. The detailed nurses with stretchers followed immediately behind the line of battle. The wounded men, if able to walk, with the permission of their company officers hurried back to the temporary depôt. Those unable to walk were carried by the nurses on the stretchers. No soldier was permitted to leave the ranks to assist the wounded, unless to carry the dead and wounded back a few yards. Temporary dressings were applied. Serious operations only were performed in extreme cases at the temporary depôt. Those unable to walk were taken in ambulances to the division hospital. There the serious work began, and was continued until the best thing possible in our surroundings was carried out for every man.[12]

The use of tents for field hospitals appeared early in the war, most notably during the Battle of Shiloh in April 1862. They proved so satisfactory that large tents were regularly issued

Field hospital for Kearney's Brigade at the Widow Allen's House, at the time of the Battle of Fair Oaks in Virginia. Fair Oaks was part of the Seven Days Battles in June, 1862, the climax of the Peninsula Campaign. The soldiers in the photo are not identified; the picture was number 442, part of a series entitled "Photographic Incidents of the War" exhibited at Gardner's Gallery (7th and D Streets, Washington, D.C.) The original negative was taken by James F. Gibson.

Hospital set up on the field at Antietam in an area known as Smoketown, on the farm of Dr. Ortho Smith, located west of Antietam Creek and one mile west of Keedysville. It was a tent hospital with a capacity of 600 beds. The Union surgeon in the picture, Dr. Anson Hurd, 14th Indiana Volunteers, was caring for Confederate wounded at the time this picture was taken.

for the purpose. Each tent could accommodate eight patients comfortably, and two or more tents could be joined to create larger units. When sufficient numbers of tents were available, surgeons rarely used the cold, dark existing buildings, even for temporary hospitals, and, when the large permanent hospitals were full, tents were added outside the main buildings to provide additional beds.[13] Special mechanisms to heat tents were designed, with the fire outside, to keep smoke from bothering the patients.

Throughout the war, line officers discouraged the transfer of men to general hospitals. If men stayed in the field hospitals, they returned to their units when they recovered. When men were sent to general hospitals in another city, the regiment rarely saw them again. Nevertheless, the number of cases in the general hospitals increased markedly as the war went on, probably resulting in part from the growing number of men suffering prolonged disabilities or slow recovery from suppurating gunshot wounds. Moreover, the enormous numbers of wounded in the later military campaigns, such as Grant's Overland Campaign of 1864, required quick transfer of the sick and wounded from the field hospitals to general hospitals in cities to free up beds in the field for new casualties.

Patients were moved from field aid stations to field hospitals, then to divisional or corps hospitals in the area of battle or encampment, and, subsequently, to hospital facilities in major army depots or nearby cities. When prolonged hospitalization seemed likely, soldiers were sent to large general or convalescent hospitals in major cities near their homes. Whenever possible, they were transported by specially designed hospital ships and, later, on newly designed hospital trains; the boats and trains were outfitted with medicines, supplies, and appropriate staff.

A Civil War hospital steward who worked as assistant at a forward aid station described the care in the field as follows:

Entrance to a field hospital at Brandy Station, VA, where much of the army, especially the cavalry, was located late in 1863 and early 1864. Near here an important cavalry battle was fought just a few weeks before Gettysburg. Brandy Station became an important base for the Army of the Potomac again during the winter of 1863–4, and was in use until the start of Grant's move south in 1864 ("The Overland Campaign).

Soldiers lined up to draw water for the hospitals set up in Fredericksburg, VA. This picture was probably taken in May 1864.

[The] emergency case or hospital knapsack was always taken with the regiment when the firing line was about to be approached, and where the First Assistant Surgeon was in charge and was ready to render first aid to any who might be wounded.

This first aid, however, never went further than stanching bleeding vessels and applying temporary dressings. Thus attended to, the wounded were taken to an ambulance, and in this conveyed to the field hospital in the rear, generally out of musket range, but almost never beyond the reach of shells and cannon balls.[14]

The picture above illustrates the difficulties in providing facilities and supplies to care for the huge numbers of wounded that overwhelmed the meager resources of the small town of Fredericksburg, Virginia. A crowd of hospital orderlies tries to get water for their hospitals from the main well in the town. Before the war began, Fredericksburg had a total population of about 5,000. After the battles of the Wilderness and Spottsylvania, in May 1864, the wounded men were moved as soon as possible by ambulance trains from the battle site field hospitals to Fredericksburg. Dr. Thomas McParlin, Medical Director of the Army of the Potomac, calculated that 21,578 wounded were cared for in Fredericksburg between May 5 and May 22.[16]

Almost all of the residences in the town were taken over as temporary hospitals, and the residents of the town, although loyal Confederates, cooperated for the most part, helping provide care for the wounded, who were mostly Union soldiers. The official report of Dr. McParlin describes what happened in Fredericksburg during this period:

. . . a series of depot hospitals had been organized at Fredericksburg by Surg. Edward B. Dalton, U.S. Volunteers, who reached that place with the first train of wounded on the 9th of May. All the churches, warehouses, and convenient dwelling-houses in the place were immediately occupied as hospitals, each corps organization being kept distinct as far as possible. The character of the buildings selected was generally good, and the ventilation sufficient, but as wounded continued to arrive in large numbers, closer packing became necessary, and the usual results of over-crowding began to be apparent. The ground occupied was elevated, well drained, and there was an abundant supply of good water. Supplies of all kinds arrived at Belle Plain on the 10th and 11th of May, and were brought to Fredericksburg as rapidly as transportation could be procured. [The schedule] appended to this report shows the character and amount of the supplies furnished by the Medical Department. The stores sent with the first train and those contained in the ambulance boxes served for the necessities of the wounded until supplies could be brought from Belle Plain. The wounded officers were at first billeted upon the inhabitants of the town, who, as a general rule, received them kindly and treated them well, although at first some of the citizens seemed inclined to make trouble. After the first week an officers' hospital was established, and medical officers specially detailed for duty in it. By the 13th, the condition of the wounded in Fredericksburg was comparatively comfortable, and the supply of all necessary articles was abundant, straw for bedding and stationery were the articles of which there was the greatest lack. The number of wounded at that date was about 6,000, but the number fluctuated almost hourly, and it was impossible to prepare accurate daily reports. The greatest want was of medical officers, those who accompanied the trains being greatly fatigued and insufficient in numbers. Fifty medical officers in all were sent from the front, being all that could possibly be spared. A number of medical men (civilians) came down from Washington as volunteers for the emergency, and rendered material and valuable assistance in a pro-fessional way, but they were for the most part ignorant of some of the most important

Drawing of field hospital on Culp's Hill during the Battle of Gettysburg.

duties of a medical officer under such circumstances, viz, to procure proper supplies; to see that his patient's food is abundant and properly served; that comfortable beds are provided, and thorough cleanliness enforced. Their attention was diverted from cases really needing their care by the loud complaints of the stragglers and malingerers with which the town was filled, and, being unfamiliar with the routine of military discipline, they could exercise no sufficient command or control over the soldiers.[17]

The drawing above shows a temporary field hospital set up on Culp's Hill during the Battle of Gettysburg. The seminary, which was the site of the first day's action, was also converted into a field hospital. The main temporary hospital at Gettysburg was some distance behind the lines; it was enlarged repeatedly until all of the wounded in the temporary hospitals, including the captured Confederates, were well enough to be moved there. It was still receiving wounded from the field hospitals in late August. It had six rows of tents, with about 400 tents in each row, arranged in streets and cross streets; the tents generally held twelve beds. Named after Medical Director Jonathan Letterman (Camp Letterman), it remained in operation until all of the wounded could be moved to permanent facilities in major towns and cities. Camp Letterman closed one day after the cemetery was dedicated (November 19), when President Lincoln made his famous "few appropriate remarks."

THE CONFEDERATE MEDICAL DEPARTMENT

Few pictures are available of the Confederate Medical Department, probably because few were taken. The staged system of care used by the Union army existed on the Confederate side, but it was less formally organized. The Confederate ambulance service also improved substantially during the war, but it was never placed under the control of the Medical Department. Field aid stations and field hospitals functioned essentially in the same fashion as in the Union Army.

The Confederate Medical Department was divided into two major divisions: the staff of the general hospitals and the staff of field hospital surgeons. Transfers of personnel occurred between the divisions, but in general they were kept separate. The field staff set up and ran a network of receiving and forwarding hospitals, established at key points, such as where evacuation routes met the railroad lines, for soldiers in transit from the battlefields to the large general hospitals. For example, a hospital was set up where the turnpike running down the Shenandoah Valley met the east–west railroad at Staunton, Virginia. General John Daniel Imboden's sad ambulance train that evacuated the wounded from Gettysburg used that route. There were also wayside hospitals along the routes used by soldiers going home on furlough or discharged for wounds or sickness.[18] Soldiers in transit received care for brief periods in these wayside hospitals—to allow them time to recover from the painful stress of the long ambulance rides and so that nurses could redress wounds, stop new bleeding, and give other forms of care. When men were able to continue their journey, they were sent by ambulance or train to general hospitals farther in the rear, primarily in Richmond in the east and Atlanta in the west.

ENDNOTES

1   *Official Records of the War of the Rebellion [O.R.],* Series I, Vol. V, p. 77. Also in: Maxwell, W. Q., *Lincoln's Fifth Wheel: The Political History of the U.S. Sanitary Commission.* New York: Longmans, Green & Co., 1956.

2   *O.R.,* Series I, Vol. XI/1, p. 210. Also in: *The Photographic History of the Civil War.* New York: Review of Reviews, 1970 (orig. pub. 1911), Vol. 4B, Appendix.

3   Billings, J. S., Medical reminiscences of the Civil War. *Journal of the Society of Civil War Surgeons.* July-Aug 1997; 6–8. *Transactions of the College of Physicians of Philadelphia,* 3rd Series, 1905; 27:115–121.

4   Duncan, L. C., *The Medical Department of the United States Army in the Civil War.* Gaithersburg, Md.: Butternut Press, 1985, p. 109.

5   Greenbie, M., *Lincoln's Daughters of Mercy,* p. 142.

6   Riley, H. D., Jr., Medicine in the Confederacy. Part 2. *Military Medicine.* 1956 Feb; 118(2):144–153.

7   Gillette, M. C., *The United States Army Medical Department, 1818–1865.* Washington, D.C.: Center of Military History, U.S. Army, 1987, p. 295.

8   *Medical and Surgical History,* Surgical Section, Vol. 3, p. 956.

9   *O.R., Series I,* Vol. XLV/1. Article 93, p. 113.

10 Ibid., Art 93, p. 139.

11 Gillett, M. C., p. 235.

12 Hart, A. G., *The Surgeon and the Hospital in the Civil War.* Gaithersberg, Md.: Olde Soldier Books, 1987, (orig. pub. 1902), p. 41.

13 Gillett, M. C., p. 290.

14 Johnson, C. B., *Muskets and Medicine, or Army life in the Sixties.* Philadelphia: F. A. Davis & Co., 1917. Quoted in: Commager, H. S., *The Blue and the Gray.* Vol. II. Indianapolis: Bobbs-Merrill, 1950, pp. 195–196.

15 Frasanito, W., *Antietam: The Photographic Legacy of America's Bloodiest Day,* 1978, New York: Charles Scribner's Sons, p. 215.

16 *O.R., Series I,* Vol. XXXVI/3. Union correspondence, orders, and returns relating to operations in southeast Virginia and North Carolina, from May 20, 1864, to June 12, 1864. Article 69, p. 146.

17 *O.R., Series I,* Vol. XXXVI/1. May 4–June 12, 1864. Campaign from the Rapidan to the James River, Va. No. 4, Reports of Surgeon Thomas A. McParlin, U.S. Army, Medical Director, including operations January 14–July 31. Article 67, pp. 234–235.

18 Wheat, T. A., Receiving and Forwarding Hospitals of the Army of Northern Virginia, Presentation at 5th Annual Conference of the Society of Civil War Surgeons, Knoxville, Tenn., March 21, 1998.

19 *O.R., Series I,* Vol. XLV/1 Article 93, p. 113.

20 Ibid., Article 93, p. 139.

21 Frasanito, W. *Antietam: The Photographic Legacy of America's Bloodiest Day.* 1978, New York: Charles Scribner's Sons, p. 215.

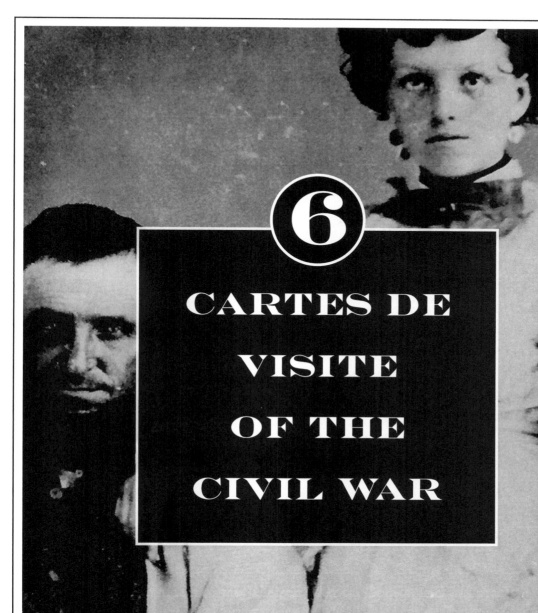

6

CARTES DE VISITE OF THE CIVIL WAR

As PHOTOGRAPHY GREW RAPIDLY IN POPULARITY, the practice of putting a person's photograph on a visiting card become common. Fortunately, this practice was widely adopted during the Civil War, and as a result, many images of Union and Confederate surgeons have been preserved.

This chapter contains *cartes des visite* (CDVs) of many Union surgeons; others are included in the chapters in which the experiences of the surgeons are discussed in some detail.

UNION SURGEONS

Born in Annapolis, Maryland, in 1828, William Hammond received his M.D. degree from the University of the City of New York (later, New York University) in 1848. After a year as house physician at the Pennsylvania Hospital and a few months in practice, he took the exam for the U.S. Army in 1849 and was appointed Assistant Surgeon. While serving on various frontier posts and at West Point, Hammond did physiological research and published several papers on nutrition. In the fall of 1859, he resigned from the army and accepted the professorship of Anatomy and Physiology at the University of Maryland in Baltimore. After the 6th Massachusetts was attacked while passing through Baltimore, Hammond attended some of their wounded at the Baltimore Infirmary. Hammond immediately resigned his professorship and reentered the army, but he had to assume the lowest rank in the medical corps, that of Assistant Surgeon.

Initially, he was appointed medical purveyor (in charge of purchasing drugs and supplies) at Frederick, Maryland. He then organized an army hospital in Baltimore before being assigned to the staff of Major General William S. Rosecrans in western Virginia as inspector of camps and hospitals. In that role, he attracted favorable attention from the U.S. Sanitary Commission, which recommended him for the position of Surgeon General. He was appointed to that post on April 25, 1862. As Surgeon General, he reformed the staff and operation of the Medical Department extensively and was responsible for most of the improvement in the performance of the Medical Department during the war. He appointed Jonathan Letterman as Medical Director of the Army of the Potomac. Hammond established the Army Medical Museum and ensured the recording and analyses of medical data in an effort to learn as much

Union Surg. General William Hammond (1862–63).

as possible from the experiences of the war. The data were ultimately published as the *Medical and Surgical History of the War of the Rebellion.*[1]

Hammond did not get along with Secretary of War Stanton, who had him removed late in 1863 by means of a court-martial based on unsubstantiated charges of improper purchasing of supplies. It seems clear, in retrospect, that Hammond, whose appointment was largely due to General McClellan, was one of the men removed after McClellan was fired as Commander of Union Army forces. Jonathan Letterman, who, as Medical Director, had been on McClellan's staff, left the Army of the Potomac in January 1864.

Dr. Joseph H. Barnes, Union Surgeon General during the last two years of the war.

Dr. Joseph H. Barnes succeeded William Hammond as Surgeon General and served for the remainder of the war and well into the 1880s. He carried on Hammond's reforms and was a good administrator. Near the end of his successful, effective tenure, he was involved in the care of the wounded President Garfield, and he was widely criticized for not using the early forms of sterile technique that had then begun to be adopted.

Surg. Samuel W. Everett, 10th Illinois, killed in action at Shiloh April 6, 1862, the first Union surgeon to die in combat in the Civil War. Tombstone marking the grave of Surg. Everett on the battlefield at Shiloh.

Surg. Thomas A. McParlin, who succeeded Jonathan Letterman as Medical Director of the Army of the Potomac at the end of 1863, and served in that capacity until the end of the war.

Surg. Gabriel Grant, who won the Medal of Honor.

Medal of Honor winner Dr. Grant seated in front of his tent.

Dr. Gabriel Grant served in the Army of the Potomac during the Peninsula Campaign. He was awarded a Medal of Honor July 21, 1897, and he is the only surgeon to receive that award. The citation reads as follows: Brigade-Surgeon Grant, at Fair Oaks, Virginia., on June 1, 1862, "removed severely wounded officers and soldiers from the field while under a heavy fire from the enemy, exposing himself beyond the call of duty, thus furnishing an example of most distinguished gallantry."*

Dr. Grant's tombstone at the Sleepy Hollow Cemetery in Tarrytown, NY, reads, "Gabriel Grant, M.D., major brigade and division surgeon, 1861–1865, War of the Rebellion."

---

*Medal of Honor citation, www.army.mil/cmh/html/moh/civwaral.html

(top) Surg John Wiley, 6th New Jersey Volunteers. (bottom) Surg. John Wiley sitting with his staff in front of his tent. He is seated, on the right. The tent can be seen at the National Museum of Civil War Medicine.

Surg. J. Ebersole, 19th Indiana.

Surgeon Ebersole is listed as the operator for eight amputations, described in text in one table in the *Medical and Surgical History*, as well as for fifteen others mentioned in a second table. One instance included the successful amputation of the entire arm, disarticulating and excising the head of the humerus, a procedure that usually resulted in a high mortality rate. The report of the case included the fact that the patient recovered at the Harewood Hospital, where the surgeon-in-charge was Dr. Reed Bontecue. Subsequently the soldier was fitted with an artificial arm—described as functioning "admirably"—that was designed by Dr. E. D. Hudson.

Surg. Robert R. McMeens of the 3rd Ohio Volunteers. Dr. McMeens reportedly died of a heart attack after the battle of Perryville, KY, in October 1862. Note the state of Ohio belt buckle.

Surg. Myron Robinson, 6th Conn. Regt., showing his epaulettes with the emblem of rank of major, and badge.

Surg. Edgar Parker on his horse, with hat braid and straps as well as the emblem of 13th Mass. Infantry for the bridle.

Surg Isaac Stearns, 22nd Mass Volunteers. Note the badge of the 5th Corps of the Army of the Potomac.

Surg. B. Rohrer, 10th Pennyslvania. Reserves.

In the summer of 1861, the 10th Pennsylvania Reserves were formally entered into Federal service as the 39th Pennsylvania Volunteer Infantry, and Dr. B. Rohrer (pictured above) was the regimental surgeon. Dr. Rohrer was stationed at Camp Pierpont, Virginia, in December, 1861, and then served during the Peninsula Campaign of 1862, at Fredericksburg in December 1862, and as surgeon of the 5th Corps General Hospital at Gettysburg. Dr. Rohrer also served at the Cuyler Hospital in Philadelphia and at Key West. He is mentioned in the *Medical and Surgical History* for his successful treatment of typhoid fever with a mild purge of calomel and a large dose of quinine, as well as with calomel and ipecacuanha (usually called "ipecac" in later years), and sips of turpentine when the patient's tongue became dry. Surgeon Rorher is also listed as performing a great many amputations (at least twelve).

CDV of Dr. J. Theodore Heard. Dr. Heard was a brigade surgeon, and later on became medical director of the 4th Corps during the Atlanta campaign.[4]

Medical Director Heard, standing, posed with members of his staff (date unknown).

At the Battle of Gettysburg, Dr. Heard was medical director of the 1st Corps of the Army of the Potomac; he stayed behind tending wounded in the town of Gettysburg while the town was occupied by Confederate forces and was highly commended for his actions. He was also highly commended by both Generals Oliver Otis Howard and D. S. Stanley for his actions during the Atlanta Campaign in the spring and summer of 1864, when he was Medical Director of the 4th Army Corps of General Sherman's army. During this campaign, he participated in the battles of Tunnel Hill, Buzzard Roost, Resaca, Calhoun, Adairsville, Kingston, Dallas, Kennesaw, and Atlanta. Subsequently, he moved north with his Corps to defend Franklin and Nashville against the attempted invasion by General John Bell Hood's army. Heard again received commendations.

Surg. Horace Gates of the 31st Iowa.

Surg. Armstrong, on his horse, posed with his wife. Surg. Armstrong was later court-martialed.

Surg. Benjamin Harrison, 47 and 48 NY Inf.

Surg. David Matthews, 143 NY Vol. Note the 12 Corps insignia (star).

Hand-tinted tintype of Surg. H. C. Barrell, 38th Ill.

Surg. H. C. Colton, 3rd New Jersey, who served on the staff of the Douglas Hospital in Washington, D.C.

Surg. Henry C. Clark, 3rd New Jersey.

Unknown New York surgeon, probably at the entrance to his own tent, standing near officer-of-the–day.

Surg. J. A. Wolf of 29th PA Vols.

Dr. Wolf served in the Union Army from the fall of 1861 until the end of the war. In April 1865, during Robert E. Lee's desperate retreat after the fall of Petersburg, leading to the surrender of the Army of Northern Virginia at Appomattox, Dr. Wolf set up a field hospital at Farmville. He treated both Union casualties and Confederate wounded who had been left behind.

Surg. Dr. Joel Morse, 52nd Ohio Volunteers.

Dr. Joel Morse served from the beginning of the war, mostly in the area around Nashville, Tenn. His reports and discussion of the cause and the autopsy findings of cases of diarrhea are quoted extensively in the *Medical and Surgical History.*

The rank of Acting Assistant Surgeon was used to designate a civilian physician hired on a contract basis, not officially in the army. The rank was also frequently used for a physician who had passed the examination for appointment into the army, but for whom a vacant position was not available at the time. The physician was put to work and paid as a civilian contract surgeon and referred as having that rank; when a vacancy arose, the appointment was made official and the term "acting" was removed.

Acting Assistant Surg. Bale who was surgeon of the prison barracks at Rock Island, IL.

Dr. Keeley served on the U.S. Military Railroad System, providing care to wounded and sick soldiers being transferred by railroad in special cars developed for the purpose during the second half of the war.

Surg. Keeley, U.S. Military Railroad System.

Surg. King, 14th Pennsylvania, with his family and hospital steward. An aide is holding his horse.

Surg. Oliver R. Rex, 33rd Ill.

Surg. George P. Rex, 33rd Ill, uncle of Surg. Oliver Rex.

The black troops, referred to as "colored" in the records of the Civil War, were placed in separate regiments with almost exclusively white officers and surgeons. They were not identified by states of origin and hence were considered regular army, referred to officially as "U.S." troops.

Surg. Lewis B. Power, of the 12 U.S. Colored Heavy Artillery.

Surg. Josiah Jordan, who was from Dover, Maine, served with the 22nd Maine Infantry Regiment and as Surgeon with the 6th U.S. Colored Troops, a unit that saw a lot of action. It served in the east, including during the Petersburg campaign, in a bloody battle at Chagffin's farm, east of Richmond, under General Butler. In that battle on September 29, 1864, of a total of 367 men, the regiment had suffered 41 killed and 160 wounded. The unit also sustained severe casualties attacking Fort Fisher, NC, and then joined Sherman's forces in that state.

Surg. Josiah Jordan

Medical Cadet George Parker, "General Hospital Washington, DC."

Medical cadets were medical students who were enlisted in the army for short periods when there was a shortage of physicians, particularly later in the war. They were designated as "medical cadets" and given a status equivalent to the cadets at West Point. Officially, they were ranked immediately below brevet second lieutenants. (Brevet ranks were temporary and did not necessarily change an officer's permanent rank.) Most of their duties resembled those of today's medical corpsmen. In the field, they assisted surgeons in forward aid stations and performed a variety of tasks in field and larger hospitals, helping during surgery, changing dressings, giving medications, and performing other nursing duties.[3] Many of these students returned to medical school, completed their education, and later served as assistant surgeons in the army before the war ended.

Surg. John Moore, Medical Director of the Army of the Tennessee.

Surg. Hayden, who was General Sheridan's staff surgeon.

Surg. William H. Heath, 2nd Mass. Dr. Heath died of disease.

Surg. William F. Edgar, who was the Medical Director at the time the western army was located at Cairo, Illinois, in 1862. The famed Mary "Mother" Bickerdyke began her career of army nursing in this facility.

Surg. Horace Potter of the 105th Illinois Volunteers, who was killed in battle outside of Atlanta in 1864.

Unidentified Union surgeon using a pocket watch to time a patient's pulse.

Surg. Jacob B. Mitchell, 5th Kentucky Cavalry. He was the Surgeon-in Charge of the 28th Corps Hospital in Marietta, GA, in 1864. The picture was taken on September 7, shortly after the fall of Atlanta.

Surg. George A. Otis, 27th Mass. Volunteers. Dr. Otis was one of the main editors of the Medical and Surgical History of the War of the Rebellion, *editing the surgical volumes and maintaining the surgical specimens in the Surgeon General's museum; he continued in that role for many years after the war.*

Surg. Jesse Wasson, who served with the 9th Iowa Cavalry and the 32nd Iowa Infantry.

Surg. George W. Stipp, who served as a Medical Inspector in the later years of the war.

Ass't Surg. Francis Labantown, with his wife; picture dated May 18, 1861.

Ass't Surg. James Cooper McGee, who served in hospitals in the Washington area. He sported a variant of the whiskers that came to be named after General Burnsides.

Medical Director McClellan. Note the plain uniform.

Surg. William J. Dale, who was Surgeon General of the State of Massachusetts.

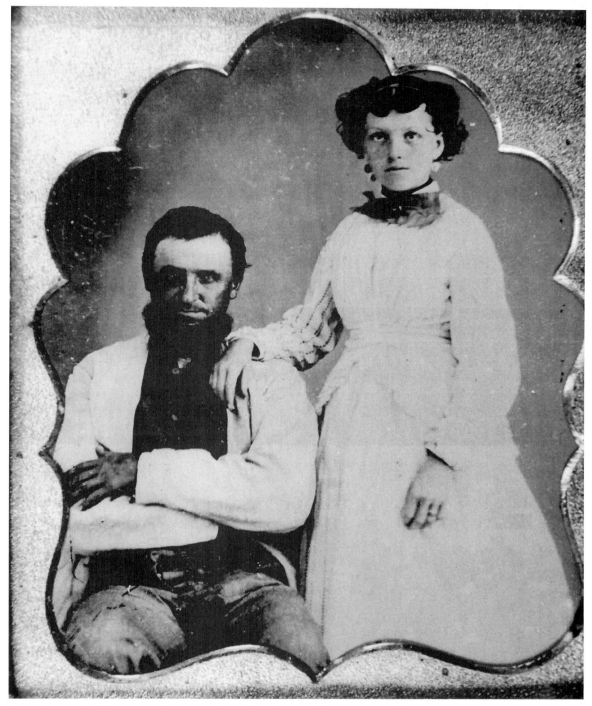

Surg. James S. O'Donnell, US Army, Purnell's Maryland Legion. Dr. O'Donnell served in the Army of the Potomac during the Battle of Antietam. The lady next to him is probably his wife.

Ass't Surg. Alfred Combs, 67th Ohio Volunteers.

Surg. John Campbell, Medical Director, Department of Susquehanna. He served in Florida for a long period beginning in May, 1861, especially at Fort Pickens on Santa Rosa Island near Pensacola. He was complimented for his quarantine measures that successfully avoided spread of yellow fever from Pensacola to Fort Pickens.

Surg. George F. Cooper, U.S. Army. Note the 20–21st century haircut.

Surg. William McKim, of the 15th Illinois Volunteers.

Surg. G. W. Briggs, who was probably from a western regiment (now called the Midwest), posed with his sword, sash and wide-brimmed hat. Surg. Briggs was specifically commended for the care of the wounded during the battle of Chancellorsville.

Unidentified Union surgeon in a photo taken in Corinth, Mississippi. Note that he is wearing the Medical Service shoulder straps with the symbol M.S.

Surg. Whipple of the 15th Wisconsin Volunteers.

Surg. A. B. Snow, 1st NY Engineers, served on Hilton Head in 1862. Note that he is holding an 1840's staff sword.

Ass't Surg. Charles A. Leale who was assigned to the Armory Square Hospital. An audience member at Ford's Theater on the evening of April 14, 1865, he was the first surgeon to gain entrance to President Lincoln's box in Ford's Theater and administer to the president at the theater and until he died across the street in a boarding house.

Unknown Union surgeon, in full uniform with his sword, in a picture taken in Portland, Maine.

Surg. Brennan, of the 5th Michigan Infantry.

Surg. Absolom B. Stuart, 1st Alabama Cavalry regiment of the Union Army.

Unidentified Union surgeon posed with his sword and sash before a painted backdrop.

Ass't Surg. J. M. Bohemier in a photo taken in Alexandria, VA.

Surg. P. D. Marshall, who served in the General Hospital at Benton Barracks in Missouri. Note the officer's walking stick.

Surg. C. H. Wilcox, 21st NY Volunteers. Dr. Wilcox served during the Second Battle of Manassas, where he was temporarily captured by the Confederates. He died of disease in November, 1862.

Surg. W.W. Holmes, 12th Ohio, very well dressed for his pose.

Surg. Joseph B. Brown, Medical Director, 4th Corps, Army of the Potomac during the Peninsular Campaign, posed with his son. Inset shows another photo of Surg. Brown.

Ass't Surg. William A. Ensign of Hatch's Independent Cavalry Battalion. Stationed mainly in Minnesota this unit was engaged primarily in actions against the Sioux Indians and guarding the frontier with British North America.

Surg. Walter K. Funderburg.

Two pictures of Surg. C. Franklin Smith, the second showing him seated at a table outside of his tent having a meal, including wine, with a companion.

A scene from Pleasant Valley, Maryland, at "Old Needwood," the home of a Mrs. Lee. Mrs. McClellan stayed here after the Battle of Antietam, which took place of September 17, 1862. The older woman in the background is probably Mrs. Lee, with Mrs. McClellan seated in front of her. The young woman on the lower step is Mary Lee, the future wife of Dr. Jonathan Letterman.

NAVAL SURGEONS

Surg. Robert Barry, U.S. Navy, in a carriage with his wife.

Surg. John J. Gibson, U.S. Navy, who served on the USS Seminole during the Battle of Mobile Bay in 1864.

Surg. Wentworth Ricker Richardson, U.S. Navy (salt print).

Surg. Andrew Coyle, U.S. Navy.

Unidentified naval surgeon.

Surg. Martin Gerould, U.S. Navy.

CONFEDERATE SURGEONS

Assistant Surg. Charles Duffy, 24th N.C. Infantry.

Note: All Confederate images courtesy of Dr. Jonathan O'Neal.

Surg. William Dearing Hoyt, 17th Georgia Infantry.

Post-war image of CSA Surgeon William Hoyle.

Confederate Surg. Deering J. Roberts, who contributed a great deal to the medical section of the Photographic History of the Civil War, *published in 1911.*

Surg. James B. Armbleton, 35th Georgia.

This photograph (above) of Confederate surgeon James B. Armbleton apparently was taken when Dr. Armbleton was held as a prisoner-of-war in Fort Warren, Mass. He is wearing some sort of improvised overcoat, apparently made from a blanket. Confederate prisoners suffered severely from the cold during the winter of 1864–65, one of the coldest on record, but had only flimsy, light clothing.

Surg. John M. Hayes of the 26th Alabama.

Confederate Surg. Robert R. Goode who was Staff Surgeon with Morgan's Cavalry.

Confederate Surg. William Post.

Surg. Robert Wilson Gibbs, who was Surgeon General of South Carolina.

Surg. Ashton Miles of the Louisiana Zoaves.

Unidentified Confederate ass't surgeon. Note the "MS" on his kepi.

Confederate Surg. Edmond Massie.

Confederate Surg. Edwin Gaillard.

ENDNOTES

1   Barnes, J. K., *Medical and Surgical History of the War of the Rebellion.* Washington, D.C.: U.S. Government Printing Office, 1870-88. [Hereafter designated as the *Medical and Surgical History*].

2   *O-R* Series. Series I, Vol. XLV/I. Article 93, p. 108.

3   U.S. Army, *Revised United States Army Regulations of* 1861. Washington, D.C.: U.S. Government Printing Office, 1863, No. 1320, p. 315.

4   *O. R.* Series. Series I, Vol. XLV/I. Article 93, p. 108.

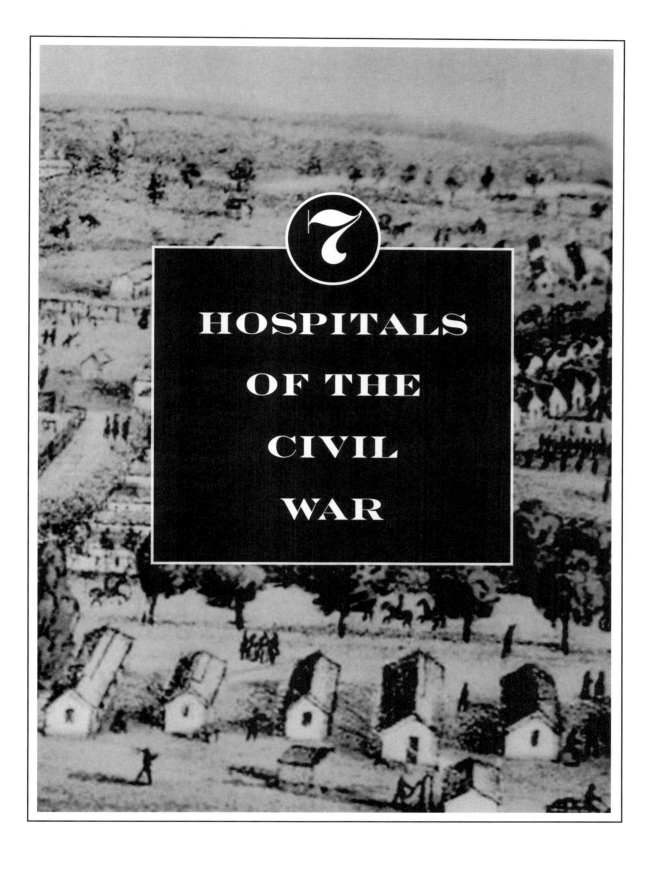

7

HOSPITALS
OF THE
CIVIL
WAR

More THAN TWO MILLION ADMISSIONS of Union and Confederate soldiers to military hospitals are recorded during the course of the war, an achievement unprecedented in size and scope. Before 1860, the U.S. Army had infirmaries at army posts, but only one was considered a hospital, a 40-bed unit at the military post at Fort Leavenworth in Kansas.[1] Despite the absence of precedents in European military facilities, both the Union and Confederate Medical Departments built and ran large general hospitals and devised new types of hospitals. They established mobile field hospitals, evacuation hospitals near the battlefront, temporary depot hospitals at transfer sites, and hospitals devoted to specific surgical specialties, as well as about 400 hundred large, fixed general hospitals, mostly in major cities. Given the availability and quality of hospital care in civilian life in the United States and Europe at the time, these were outstanding achievements. Records show that, of the one million patients cared for in Federal hospitals over the course of the war, *fewer than 10 percent died*. The Confederates had similar accomplishments. The mortality figures available for Confederate hospitals seem a bit lower. However, these figures may be, in part, because of a system of counting transfers to a new unit within a hospital as a new admission, thereby inflating figures for total admissions.

The problems that the staffs of the Medical Departments faced were immense. At the outbreak of hostilities, the only military hospital in Washington was a six-room, two-story brick structure used to isolate smallpox patients.[2] Civilian hospitals everywhere were primarily institutions for the indigent sick, and a few were still evolving from infirmaries attached to poorhouses. Sick people were treated at home, if they had a home. After a bumbling start, because of incompetent leadership based on seniority in the Union Army, the medical staffs of the Civil War determined a good plan for design and construction of the needed hospital facilities. They also provided enormous numbers of patients with food, medicines, medical and nursing care, and invented the type of treatment now called rehabilitation.

EVOLUTION OF GENERAL HOSPITALS

Early in the war, both sides employed a variety of existing structures as field hospitals and in cities, fixed general hospitals. Public buildings, hotels, churches, schools, warehouses, mills, and private homes were pressed into service after a battle. In May 1861, even the partially completed Capitol building in Washington was used as a barracks and hospital; about 2,000 men lying on cots and mattresses lined the rotunda, halls, and various committee rooms and offices. The buildings of the Naval Academy at Annapolis and those on the grounds of the Agricultural Society of Frederick County were converted to hospital uses early in the war.[3] Baltimore contained a couple of notable instances of extemporized hospital accommodations, including the National Hotel and West's warehouses.

Civilian institutions were woefully inappropriate for hospital use, lacking sufficient toilets or provision for bathing, facilities that could serve as a mortuary, and, in the case of most churches, adequate heating. Former hotels had tortuous corridors, could not be properly cleaned, and required extra staffing. Contemporaries complained of poor ventilation, fearing the spread of disease by "miasmas," but the overwhelmingly sickening odors and stifling heat were reasons enough to complain.

In general, officers were supposed to provide for their own care, and they frequently obtained it in private homes. This system mirrored the civilian system of providing medical, obstetrical, and even surgical care in a domestic setting for people who were relatively well-off. Confederate officers were often able to receive care in the homes of friends in the neighborhood of a battle.

Initially, most of the small regimental hospitals in the training camps were tents. The use of tents for field hospitals started early in the war, especially during the Battle of Shiloh in April 1862. They proved so satisfactory that large tents were issued for the purpose and widely used. These tents accommodated eight patients comfortably, and two or more tents could be joined to create larger units.[4] When tents were available, surgeons rarely used the cold, dark hotels and churches, even for temporary field hospitals. When the beds in the fixed general hospitals became filled, large numbers of tents were added outside the main buildings to provide additional beds.

Huge tent complexes arose, arranged militarily in orderly columns and rows. During the crisis caused by the huge numbers of wounded and sick evacuated from Virginia after the Peninsula campaign in mid-1862, the U.S. Sanitary Commission erected about 1,000 hospital tents around the White House.[5] Tents were also used to isolate patients thought to have contagious diseases, thus minimizing the spread of hospital gangrene and erysipelas. They also served as "pest hospitals" for smallpox patients. Ventilation in tents was excellent, and effective heating systems were devised.

At first, solid red flags were used to mark field hospitals; after 1863, hospital tents were marked by yellow flags with a green "H" in the center. When field hospitals were overrun by advancing enemy forces, these flags identified them, protecting their occupants and staff.

Both Union and Confederate armies developed an innovative type of hospital construction. The fixed hospitals were built pavilion-style out of wood, with multiple single-story, barracks-like ward units arranged in columns or in rows. These wards generally formed either a grid or an arc, with a central administrative facility. Typical pavilion units were 150 feet long and 25 feet wide, with 12- to 14-foot ceilings,[6] according to a plan originated in the Surgeon General's Office by Dr. John Shaw Billings,[7] who later in the century designed the Johns Hopkins Hospital. These ward units were inexpensive and could be erected quickly where needed; some of them remained in use long after the war, including, in 1890, the Lincoln and Harewood Hospitals in Washington, the Sedgewick Hospital in New Orleans, and the Hicks Hospital in Baltimore. A similar type of construction continued to be used for temporary or semipermanent military hospitals throughout World War I and even during and after World War II.

Individual hospital pavilions usually contained about sixty beds and were abundantly fitted with windows, in accordance with the designs suggestion by Florence Nightingale, who emphasized the need for maximum ventilation based on her experiences in the Crimean War.[8] Consequently, they were drafty and often quite cold in winter.[9] The draftiness actually was considered beneficial, because it carried away the almost constant, often overwhelming odors of pus and putrefying tissue and hence removed "miasmas." The mode of construction allowed for swift completion of hospitals. For example, a contractor in Philadelphia agreed to provide a functional hospital of 2,500 beds in forty days. Although not entirely completed, the Satterlee Hospital opened on the appointed date and was later expanded to 3,500 beds.[10]

Many of the general hospitals were in operation for only part of the war, particularly those in relatively remote areas where major battles had occurred. A total of 431 institutions are listed in the archives of the Adjutant General's Office. However, during the last year of the war, the number of general hospitals in operation at any one time probably peaked at 204.[11] During that last year, the average number of patients in Union hospitals peaked at 71,484. There were also convalescent centers with more than 21,000 beds, mainly near Washington.[12]

WASHINGTON, D.C. AREA HOSPITALS

During the war, about twenty-eight military hospitals were set up in Washington and several more were established in nearby areas, including six in Georgetown and five in the Alexandria area. The largest were the Lincoln Hospital in southwest Washington and the Armory Square Hospital, near the Capitol.[13] The Lincoln Hospital held as many as 2,575 beds (including beds in tents) and treated a total of about 46,000 patients; in 1890, it still contained 1,240 beds.[14] Many of these temporary Civil War hospitals were still in use in 1890, including the Lincoln and Harewood Hospitals in Washington.

The description of Armory Square Hospital in the *Medical and Surgical History of the War of the Rebellion* illustrates the factors that were considered in selecting a site for a hospital. Also noteworthy are the provisions made for private facilities for female nurses, a subject discussed in more detail later.

The Armory Square Hospital, Washington, D.C., was constructed during the summer of 1862, after plans furnished by Ass't Surgeon J. J. Woodward, U.S. Army [who worked in the Surgeon General's Office]. It was situated on Seventh Street

Medical staff of the Lincoln Hospital, Washington, D.C.

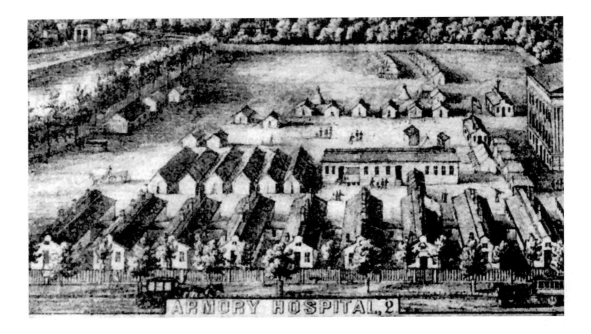

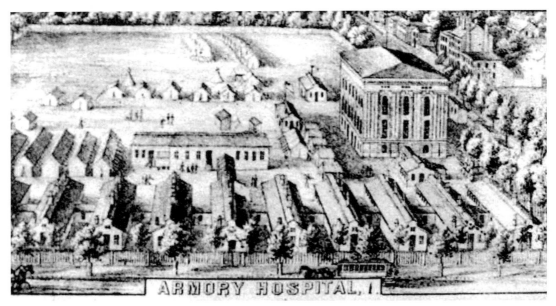

Two views of Armory Hospital, usually called the Armory Square Hospital. It was located opposite the grounds of the Smithsonian Institution, in view of the Capitol. (Lithographed postal envelopes, from the collection of F. Terry Hambrecht, M.D.)

opposite the grounds of the Smithsonian Institution, and just beyond the canal which, at that time, was an open sewer reeking with the filth of the city, rendered the location unwholesome. This site was selected on account of its proximity to the great thoroughfares and its easy access from the wharves and railroad depot.

The hospital consisted of eleven long pavilions placed parallel to each other, with their gables facing the front and rear of the grounds. Adjacent pavilions were separated by a space no wider than the width of one of the buildings. The central pavilion constituted the administration building; the others, five on each side, were used as wards. The central building contained a reception room, from which a passage continued through the center of the length of the building, with small rooms on either side used as the office of the surgeon in charge, the dispensary, general office, linen-room, post-office, store-room and officers' quarters and mess-room. In rear of the central building and connected with it by a covered way was the general kitchen, 105 × 25 feet, and the laundry, 47 × 17 feet; a bakery, 36 × 16 feet, was a subsequent addition.

On the right flank, near the stable and knapsack-room, . . . a chapel and chaplain's quarters, rooms for female nurses and a dead-house were afterwards constructed. In the rear of the kitchen and laundry, and between them and the guard-house, two barrack-buildings were erected, one for contrabands, the other for the guard. On the left flank of the hospital was the Columbian Arsenal, a three-story brick building 103 × 57 feet, the rooms of which were fitted up as wards to increase the capacity of the hospital.

Each pavilion-ward was 149 × 25 feet with an average height of about 13 feet, and accommodated 50 beds; one on the left of the line was somewhat shorter than the others on account of the position of neighboring buildings. A portion of the rear end of each ward was used as a dining-room; before separate quarters were provided for the female nurses this room was so partitioned as to afford them a lodging. At the other extremity of the ward were the bath-room, water-closet and wardmaster's room. The buildings were connected by a continuous covered-way along their rear and by transverse passages between adjacent wards near the middle of their length. The capacity of this hospital was occasionally increased by the use of tent-wards. Ventilation was by the ridge, shafts and floor-inlets, as was usual in the pavilions built at this period.[15]

U.S. Patent Office Building, Washington, D.C. (Bell & Bro. Washington, D.C. From the collection of F. Terry Hambrecht, M.D.)

Called in the Official Records the "Patent Office Hospital," it was used as a hospital early in the war. Sick and injured soldiers initially were housed on cots amid models of patented inventions until several floors were cleared out for hospital use. Clara Barton worked as a clerk in the Patent Office when the war began.

OTHER HOSPITALS IN THE WASHINGTON, D.C. AREA

The Finley Hospital had 1,061 beds; the Medical Officer in Charge was Surgeon O. L. Pancoast. The hospital was named after the physician who became Surgeon General at the start of the war; promoted because of seniority and used to a tiny peacetime army, Finley was not up to the wartime job and was relieved of it in April 1862.

The central facility of Mount Pleasant Hospital consisted of ten pavilions attached to a central corridor, allowing complete communication with each other through the central corridor. The facility remained in use as a Veterans Administration Hospital for a long time. Note also in the illustrations on page 120 the large number of hospital tents. The hospital had 1,618 beds. Assistant Surgeon H. Allen, U.S. Army, was listed as Medical Officer-in-Charge.

Picture showing Ward A of Finley Hospital, Washington, D.C., with the attendants posed in front of it.

Surg. J. Penfield Weyer, who served on the staff of the Mount Pleasant Hospital.

Two views of Mount Pleasant Hospital in Washington, D.C.

Campbell General Hospital, Washington, D.C., showing pavilions arranged around the sides of a hollow square.[16]

The arrangement of the pavilions of Campbell General Hospital around the sides of a hollow square had been used in several other hospitals but was deemed unsatisfactory because it interfered with ventilation.[16] In December, 1864, the hospital had 900 beds; Surgeon A. F. Sheldon, U.S. Volunteers, was listed as Medical Officer in Charge. The Campbell Hospital was located on the northern outskirt of the city, near Seventh Street. It was described in the *Medical and Surgical History* as follows:

[It] consisted of long, low, narrow buildings of rough boards, originally used as barracks for cavalry. Six of these enclosed an oblong space having two buildings on

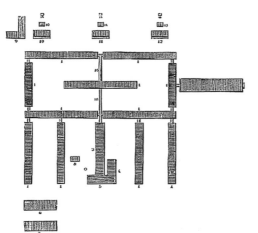

Ground plan of the Campbell Hospital [from the Medical and Surgical History].[18] *Note that building number 11 was allocated to nurses' quarters, complying with the requirement that newly constructed hospitals have a separate facility for female nurses.*

Cliffburne Hospital in Washington, D.C.

each long side and one on each short side of the enclosure. In its centre was a seventh building with its long axis parallel to that of the oblong; these were all used as wards. Projecting perpendicularly from the two buildings, forming one of the long sides, were five buildings, that in the centre being used as a dining-room and kitchen and the others as wards. Projecting similarly from one of the short sides was the building used for administration purposes. There were thus eleven barrack-wards having an aggregate capacity of six hundred beds. Ridge ventilation was introduced when the barracks were turned over to the Medical Department.

Ten tent-wards of fifty beds each were subsequently added. This establishment was better supplied with water than the other converted barracks in the vicinity of Washington since Potomac River water was distributed to the wards. Waste-water was carried off by drains to the sewers. Every alternate ward had a water-closet and bathroom, and the sinks for convalescents were kept clean by a running stream.[17]

Also referred to in the records as Camp Cliffburne and Cliffburne Barracks, this facility was used to house and organize newly formed army units, but, early in 1862, much of the facility was converted to a hospital. Unfortunately, the area chosen had been previously used by the 5th U.S. Cavalry; according to a report by Surgeon John Shaw Billings, the area needed extensive cleaning ("Fifteen hundred loads of offal were cleared from the grounds and vicinity of the buildings. . . ."). After additional buildings were added, along with 105 hospital tents, it had facilities for 1,000 patients.[19]

Unknown hospital under construction next to a hotel or apartment facility that was probably being used as a hospital, in Washington, D.C.

Columbia College and Carver Barracks Hospitals. Carver Hospital had 1,300 beds; the Medical Officer-in-Charge was Surg. O. A. Judson. Columbia Hospital had 844 beds; the Medical Officer in Charge was T. R. Crosby.

Harewood Hospital had about 900 beds, and at one time, as many as 312 regulation hospital-tents were pitched on the grounds of this hospital. The tents were arranged in thirteen divisions, six pavilions to a division and four tents to each pavilion. Each tent accommodated six men; thus 1,872 beds were added altogether, twice the number in the original hospital.

The Harewood Hospital, was described in the *Medical and Surgical History* as follows:

> . . . situated on what was known as the Corcoran farm on the Seventh street road, near the Soldiers' Home. The ground was gently rolling and diversified with woodlands and cultivated fields. The pavilions, of unplaned boards, were arranged en echelon in two lines, meeting at an acute angle, with the administration building placed lengthwise at this point. The wards in their position posterior and external to this building were parallel with it. Six were thus disposed on the right and rear of the administration building and nine on the other retiring line. The kitchens and dining-rooms were within the space bounded by the lines of the pavilions, and facilities were afforded for communication between the various buildings by means of covered foot-ways. Each ward, 187 × 24 × 16 feet to the eaves and 20 feet to the ridge, contained 63 beds. The out-buildings in the hospital complex included one building designated as "quarters for female nurses."[20]

Dr. Bontecue served with the Army of the Potomac and treated the wounded from the Peninsula Campaign of spring 1862 (where he served at the Hygeia and Chesapeake Hospitals at Fort Monroe) to the siege of Petersburg in 1864; subsequently, he served as Medical Officer in Charge at the Harewood Hospital in Washington, D.C. in 1865 and 1866. Dr. Bontecue reported more than 200 cases and surgical procedures that were published in the *Medical and Surgical History*. Some were skull injuries in which he had to trephine the skull in order to release intracranial pus; however, the outcome in all of these cases was fatal.

Dr. Bontecue's army experiences included participation in the attack on Fort Wagner, near Charleston, in July, 1863, taking many of the wounded by boat from Folly Island, where the assault took place, to Hilton Head and Beaufort. He was subsequently in charge of Hospital Number One in Beaufort.

Harewood Hospital in northwest Washington, D.C. near the Old Soldiers Home and not far from Fort Stevens (where Lincoln was under fire during the invasion of Maryland in 1864 by Confederate General Jubal Early).

Surg. Bontecue and other staff at the hospital in Fortress Monroe at the tip of the York-James Peninsula, Virginia, probably taken at the start of the Peninsula Campaign in 1862.

Surg. Bontecue and an unidentified person walking near the Harewood Hospital early in 1864.

Surg. Bontecue and staff with wives, on an outing.

House used by Surg. Bontecue while he served as Medical Officer-in-Charge at Harewood Hospital.

Photo of a pet dog at the Harewood Hospital in Washington, D.C.

Surg. Reed Bontecue, chief surgeon at Harewood Hospital between 1863 and 1866.

Soldiers' Home in northwest Washington, D.C. The building served as a hospital for Civil War veterans and later as a home for veterans in general.

Drawing of the Soldiers' Home

The Soldier's Home was in northwest Washington, D.C., near the site of the Harewood Hospital. It continued in use as a retirement home for service personnel, as it is to this day. President Lincoln moved with his family to a home there during the summers to avoid the heat of downtown Washington. He commuted to work at the White House by horseback each morning, often unaccompanied, and was observed—by Walt Whitman on at least one occasion—riding to the White House.

Slough Hospital, Alexandria. This hospital definitely existed, at least in 1864 and 1865, but we have found no information about it. This photograph shows the typical pavilion construction; the two-storied building was probably for administration and housing of the staff.

Surgeons and staff posed in front of house used as a hospital in Fairfax, Virginia.

The Seminary Hospital in Fairfax had 936 beds; in December 1864, the Medical Officer-in-Charge was Surgeon D. P. Smith. This house may have been part of the hospital or a residence for staff of the hospital.

Staff posed at entrance to Seminary Hospital, Fairfax, Virginia.

PHILADELPHIA HOSPITALS

Satterlee Hospital in Philadelphia.

Before the war, Dr. Satterlee was a senior member of the Medical Department of the Army and was the Chief Medical Purveyor in New York City, in charge of obtaining drugs and supplies from the northeastern states. In one of the early actions taken after being appointed Surgeon General in April, 1862, Surgeon General Hammond arranged for the construction of the first large new hospital facility for the army in Philadelphia. He named it for Dr. Satterlee. Surgeon I. Hayes, appointed as Surgeon-in-Charge, made the following report about the speedy start-up and operation of the Satterlee Hospital on October 31, 1862:

This hospital was commenced May 1, 1862, and by the terms of the contract was to have been completed in forty days. Seven of the wards were ready for use on the 6th of June, and, as ordered, I proceeded to organize the hospital and prepare it for the reception of patients. On the 9th the completed wards were filled with patients, and the other wards were occupied as rapidly as finished. I was fortunate in being able to engage, as directed when the hospital was first opened, forty Sisters of Charity, whose labors have been unceasing and valuable. I enlisted also a sufficient number of hospital attendants, allowing eleven to each hundred patients. Many students of medicine volunteered their assistance and were placed on duty as acting medical cadets. This useful body of young men, performing duty without pay, at one time numbered as many as 41. The medical staff was enlarged as

Surg. Richard Smith Satterlee.

the hospital filled up, and at present there are 35 medical officers on duty, exclusive of 18 cadets. There are now thirty-six wards in the hospital, twenty-eight in the house and eight in the hospital camp [the tents]. The personnel of each ward comprises a surgeon, a Sister of Charity, a wardmaster and three nurses. . . . The hospital is located at the intersection of 44th and Spruce streets, a half mile outside of the present city limits, west of what is known as West Philadelphia.[21]

There is no record of a West End Hospital in the official records of the war. Because the Satterlee Hospital was located in West Philadelphia and underwent several name changes during the war, this probably was the Satterlee.

Another view of Satterlee Hospital. At the top is an enlarged detail showing the arrangement of buildings. This engraving was printed on the back of the menu for the Christmas Dinner, 1864, served to hospitalized soldiers in Philadelphia. This dinner was hosted by Mrs. E. C. Egbert, wife of Dr. M. C. Egbert. Other prints of this engraving also identify it as West End Hospital, Philadelphia. (From the collection of F. Terry Hambrecht, M.D.)

The Christian Street Hospital, Philadelphia, opened in June, 1861, was the only general hospital in that city for several months. When the Army of the Potomac was preparing to leave its training sites and start the campaign of 1862, increased accommodations were required in Philadelphia. Brigade and regimental hospitals were disbanded, and their patients were moved northward. A number of buildings were hastily transformed into hospitals, all of which were at first considered wards of the military hospital at Philadelphia, with headquarters in a hospital building at Broad and Cherry Streets. A ward at this site was located at the railroad depot and thus served as the admitting ward for the general hospital. The hospital at the Christian Street building was previously a commissioners' hall; a unit established at Fifth and Buttonwood was a coach factory; one at Twenty-Fourth and South Streets was a silk factory; in addition, an old arsenal at Sixteenth and Filbert was converted to a hospital. In a few months, "The Philadelphia Hospital" was reorganized and each of the establishments, hitherto its wards, became separate general hospitals.

CONVALESCENT HOSPITALS

There were several convalescent hospitals, in different locales, where soldiers were sent who needed prolonged recovery before being discharged, returned to duty, or transferred to the limited duty Veterans Reserve Corps (originally called the Invalid Corps). The convalescent hospital in Alexandria was the largest, with 668 beds late in the war.

Convalescent Hospital, Alexandria, Virginia.
From Harper's Weekly.

Another image of "Camp Convalescent" (sometimes called "Camp Misery").

The convalescent hospital in the Alexandria, Virginia, area was officially called a "Rendez-vous of Distribution." Officially it was "Camp Convalescent," but the men called it "Camp Misery." The hospital accommodated disabled soldiers awaiting recovery and reassignment or discharge. It also housed new recruits waiting for their assignments, exchanged prisoners of war, and captured deserters and stragglers awaiting final disposition of their cases. The first soldiers' newspaper, the *Soldiers' Journal*, was started there, a forerunner of the newspaper *Yank* of World War II fame.[22]

The depot hospitals were set up, primarily by the U.S. Sanitary Commission, in several cities, primarily in Philadelphia and New York City; the one shown in the illustration was probably the one in New York. Soldiers stayed in these facilities while traveling to their homes on leave or after discharge from the army. They were given a place to stay, to receive treatment of their wounds, or recover from the effects of their travel. Relatively luxurious accommodations were provided, with bathing facilities and a dining hall. A waiter providing private service is shown in the illustration on the following page; other illustrations show bootblacks.

"Refreshment Saloon" for Union soldiers in Philadelphia. Facilities such as this were run by volunteers and, like the U.S.O. facilities set up around the country during World War II, they served off-duty and traveling soldiers.

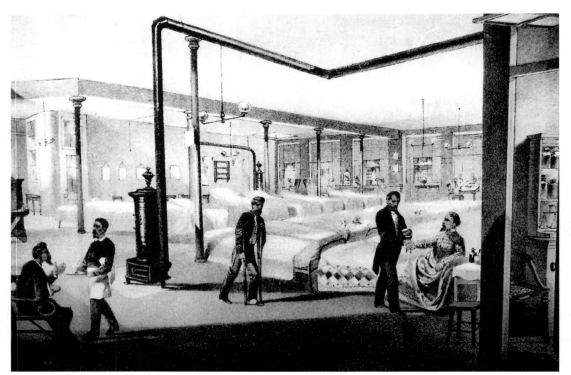

Scene on the fourth floor of a Soldiers' Depot Hospital.

OTHER GENERAL HOSPITALS

The U.S. Army General Hospital in Frederick, Maryland, sometimes referred to as "hospital number 1, Frederick," was also called the "Hessian Barracks," probably because the facility was occupied by Hessian mercenaries during the Revolutionary War. Some buildings still stand today.

A hospital was established in Frederick before the battle of Antietam; the image above is probably a picture of that institution. The Confederate Army had passed through the area before the battle; their movement through the town was commemorated by a poem and a play about their confrontation with Barbara Frietchie.[23] Medical Director Jonathan Letterman found the hospital full of Confederate wounded when he arrived with the Army of the Potomac before the battle. The hospital also treated large numbers of Confederate wounded during General Early's raid into Maryland in 1864.

Drawing of a hospital in Frederick, Maryland.

City Point Hospital (from Medical and Surgical History of the War of the Rebellion, Plate 126.)

Surgeons and chaplains at City Point Hospital.

City Point, on the James River, was the base and supply depot for the Army of the Potomac during the prolonged siege of Petersburg in 1864–65. A hospital, consisting mainly of tents, was established there, and patients were evacuated from field hospitals located just behind the Union Army trenches by means of a railroad that ran parallel to the lines. Patients were taken from the hospital at City Point up Chesapeake Bay by boat to Annapolis, Washington, and cities farther north.

General Hospital at City Point, Virginia. (From the Photographic History of the Civil War, 1861–65. From the collection of F. Terry Hambrecht, M.D.)

The ground plan of the DeCamp General Hospital reveals several features worthy of comment. It had a dock for movement of patients and supplies from New Rochelle to the island, formerly owned by a man named Davids. There was a separate facility for smallpox patients, located on the opposite side of the island from the main dock, and a second dock was established near it so that the patients with this contagious disease would not have to be transported

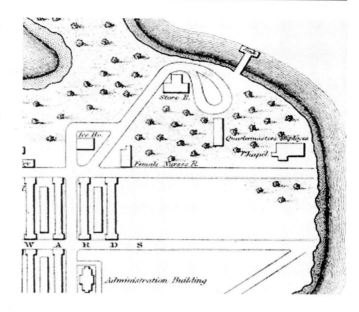

through the area housing other patients. The ground plan also shows a separate residence for female nurses, as required by regulations (as shown in the close-up).

Confederate soldiers wounded at Gettysburg and too severely ill to be taken south when Lee's army evacuated the area were moved to DeCamp Hospital after they had recovered sufficiently to travel. Unfortunately, after they recovered, they were transferred to the prisoner-of-war camp at Elmira. New York, which has been called the worst prison on both sides during the war and may have had the highest mortality rate among prisoners.

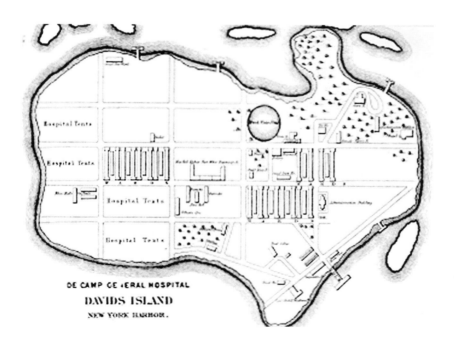

DE CAMP GENERAL HOSPITAL

DAVIDS ISLAND

NEW YORK HARBOR.

The DeCamp General Hospital was located on Davids' Island in Long Island Sound, in New Rochelle Harbor, near New York City.

Two views of USA General Hospital, Patterson Park, Baltimore Maryland. (From the collection of F. Terry Hambrecht, M.D.)

HOSPITALS IN MEMPHIS

Memphis, once taken by the Federal forces, served as main base for the operations in Mississippi against Vicksburg, Jackson, and Port Hudson in that state. Casualties from the prolonged siege of Vicksburg and fighting further south, were evacuated once they were able to travel, mainly by hospital boat up the Mississippi River to Memphis, requiring a large number of military hospitals in that city. Hospital boats were also used to transport patients from Memphis, especially to St. Louis in Missouri, and to Cairo and Mound City in Illinois. One of the hospital transport boats was named the *City of Memphis*.

Some of these hospitals were set up in pre-existing buildings with cast iron exteriors, a style of architecture that became popular around the 1850s. It was used primarily for commercial buildings, such as factories and warehouses.

Webster Hospital, Memphis, TN. The hospital had 500 beds; the Medical Officer in Charge was Surg. J. L. Teed.

Gayoso U.S. Military Hospital, Memphis, Tennessee. This hospital had 400 beds; Surg. F. N. Burke, U. S. V. was listed as Medical Officer in Charge. In December 1864, 226 of these beds were listed as vacant.

Officers Hospital, Memphis, Tennessee. This hospital with 100 beds was devoted exclusively to care of officers.

Excavation for construction of a military hospital in Memphis.

The Washington U.S. Military Hospital in Memphis, apparently in a building that had been a candy manufacturing facility. This hospital had 400 beds and was run by a contract physician, listed as Act. Assistant Surg. E. C. Strode.

Described on the records of the photograph as "Union U.S. Military Hospital, Memphis Tennessee," the full name of the hospital is not known.

Adams U.S. Military Hospital in Memphis.

The Jackson U.S. Military Hospital in Memphis, apparently established in a dry goods warehouse. It was very active in 1863 but is not listed as in operation in December, 1864.

The Jefferson U.S. Military Hospital in Memphis. This hospital was also established in a factory building and was active in 1863.

Overton U.S. Military Hospital in Memphis. In October 1862.

Photo of Surg. William P. Bailey who served in one of the military hospitals in Memphis.

In October 1862, General Sherman enlarged the Overton U.S. Military Hospital to 1,000 beds in anticipation of the Vicksburg campaign.[24] On December 17, 1864, after the action had shifted farther east and south, the hospital was listed as containing 450 beds, with Assistant Surgeon J. C. G. Happersett as the Medical Officer-in-Charge.

Dr. William P. Bailey served throughout the war, and favorable comments about his work appear in the *Official Records* beginning in September 1861. Initially he was complimented for his efforts in the field after the fighting at Lexington, Missouri, in the report by Brigadier General Thomas Harris to Major General Sterling Price. In October 1861, Bailey was serving as an Assistant Surgeon in a hospital in St. Louis where his work was complimented by Major General J. C. Fremont.

OTHER FEDERAL MILITARY HOSPITALS

Hilton Head Island was captured by an amphibious force early in November 1861; it became the main Federal base for the blockade of the Carolina and Georgia coasts, including Charleston and Savannah. It also served as the base for operations to strike inland and for the efforts to take Charleston and its surrounding islands.

The hospital was organized on March 1, 1862, and it remained in operation until October 12, 1866. Originally, it functioned in an old building that had been used as a hospital by Confederate troops. New construction was added, and, in December 1864, it was listed as containing 460 beds. The Medical Officer in Charge was Assistant Surgeon John F. Huber. Clara Barton served as a nurse at this hospital for a long period in 1863 and 1864, at one point caring for casualties from the attempts to take the forts around Charleston Harbor.

The hospital was situated on the seashore on a sandy loam, formerly a cotton field. There were swampy areas around it that were considered "malarial," and they were laboriously cleared.

The hospital on Hilton Head Island in South Carolina.

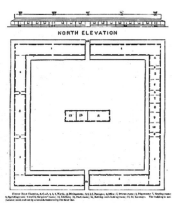

Plan of the hospital on Hilton Head Island.[25]

House used as hospital in Beaufort, South Carolina.

The building, under a continuous roof, formed the four sides of a hollow square, forming an enclosed yard. Each side was 325 feet in length. The floors were raised about three feet from the sandy ground, and a wide veranda along both the exterior and the interior of the building afforded shelter from the hot summer sun and from rain. Water was obtained from numerous wells within the enclosure. Latrines, established along the beach, were cleaned by the tide twice a day.

In December 1864, the U.S. General Hospital in Beaufort was listed as having 320 beds, and the Medical Officer in Charge was Surgeon John Treanor, Jr., U.S. Volunteers. Numerous Union Army "Colored Troops," such as the famed 54th Massachusetts regiment depicted in the motion picture *Glory*, served in this area, and a separate hospital was established for them in Beaufort in a building such as the one shown. General Hospital No. 10 was listed as the hospital for the "Colored Troops," but it is not certain if it is the one in the preceding picture.

House used by a post surgeon named Cooley in Beaufort, SC.

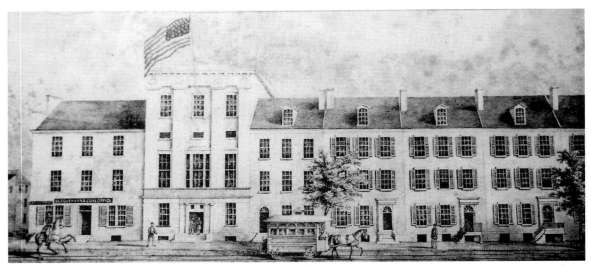

Hospital established in Newton University, Baltimore Maryland. The hospital is listed as having 260 beds on December 17, 1864, and Surg. R.W. Pease was in charge.[26]

Chesapeake Hospital, in the area of Norfolk Virginia. The label on this picture states that it was located between Fortress Monroe and Hampton, Virginia, opposite Norfolk. It was the Chesapeake Female Seminary, converted to hospital use very early in the war.

New Haven Hospital, Connecticut.

Hospitals were established in many northern cities so that wounded soldiers requiring long periods of recuperation could be near their homes. The institution in New Haven, shown in the photograph above, was called the Knight Hospital; it functioned from June 9, 1862, to November, 1865. The hospital was named for Professor J. Knight of Yale College Medical School. In December 1864, it was listed as having 607 beds, 510 of which were occupied. The Medical Officer in Charge was Surgeon P. A. Jewett, U.S. Volunteers.

House and church used as a hospital in Murfreesboro, Tennessee. In December 1864, the U.S. General Hospital in Murfreesboro had 458 beds; the Medical Officer in Charge was Surg. S. D. Turney.

A regimental band on the grounds of the U.S. Army General Hospital, Cleveland Ohio. It had 330 beds, and the Medical Officer in Charge was George M. Sternberg, who became Surgeon General in 1893, and served in that post during the Spanish-American War. He assigned Dr. Water Reed to the study of the mode of transmission of yellow fever in Cuba.

Harvey Hospital, in Madison, Wisconsin. It had 592 beds, all filled in December 1864. The Medical Officer in Charge was Surg. H. Culbertson, many of whose case reports were published in the Medical and Surgical History.

A view of a Civil War hospital in York, Pennsylvania.

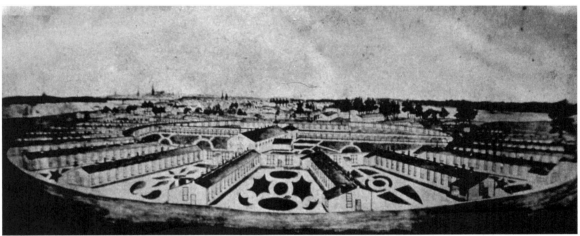

Jefferson Hospital in Indiana. (Photos of four nurses who served there are in the chapter on nursing.)

CONFEDERATE HOSPITALS

D r. Samuel P. Moore, the Confederate Surgeon General, recorded that after First Manassas (Bull Run) in July 1861, Richmond was overwhelmed with wounded and sick soldiers. The lack of facilities was aggravated when General Joseph Johnston notified the Surgeon General soon after the battle that he was clearing all of his field hospitals of sick and wounded in preparation for renewed fighting. Moore sought hospital facilities in Richmond, but the only suitable structure he found, the old "almshouse," was already filled with captured Union wounded. As a result, Confederate sick and wounded sent to Richmond from Manassas were scattered throughout the city, treated in private houses, unoccupied wooden buildings, and small tobacco factories converted into improvised hospitals. Records were poorly kept, and the army did not know the whereabouts of many of the wounded.

After this experience, the Confederate Army quickly adopted a plan to erect large hospitals and used the hospital construction plan throughout the war. It consisted of separate barracks-like structures, similar in design to those erected by the Federal authorities. The hospitals consisted of numerous small pavilions that could accommodate thirty-two beds each, with passages between the buildings. The limited size of the units kept men separated into small groups, which minimized the spread of communicable diseases. Also, similar to the Federal arrangements, men with hospital gangrene were removed from the wards and isolated in tents in an attempt to prevent spread of the disease. They also had separate "pest houses" for smallpox patients.

The Confederate Medical Department was divided into two major divisions: the staff of the general hospitals and the field hospital surgeons [The organization is described in Chapter 5, "Ambulances and Field Hospitals," page 63].

There are records of at least 154 military general hospitals set up in the Confederacy during the war. Large general hospitals were established in Richmond and other major cities, particularly in Virginia, North Carolina, Tennessee, northern Georgia, Alabama, and Mississippi, near sites of major fighting. Some, such as the one in Charlottesville, were spread among a large number of existing buildings—including homes, churches, and public buildings, as well as tents. The existing records of the medical problems and treatments for patients in the major Confederate hospitals are indistinguishable from similar records of their Union counterparts.[28]

The builders of the hospitals used untreated wood intended for tobacco processing factories, because tobacco was no longer being shipped, with most of the labor provided by the

Some of the wards of Chimborazo Hospital, built just outside of Richmond.

unemployed tobacco workers. The inexpensive nature of the construction used by both sides permitted hospitals to be built rapidly, another important attribute during wartime. Moore noted that if a hospital unit had to be abandoned because the Confederate Army withdrew from an area, such as Tennessee, it could be replaced with little cost. However, because the Confederate Medical Department was not an independent bureau and had to depend on the Quartermaster's and Commissary Departments, there could be delays in constructing and furnishing the hospital units. Moore claimed that the Medical Department received the blame for the delays, "which it never deserved."[29]

Moore had a pavilion-style hospital built on Chimborazo Hill, just outside of Richmond. Chimborazo Hospital was spread over forty acres; by the end of the war it had 150 wards, separate small buildings with forty to sixty patients each. It was probably the largest military hospital in the world then and for a long time thereafter. A total of about 58,000 sick and 17,000 wounded soldiers were treated at Chimborazo Hospital during the course of the war; just over 9 percent of its recorded admissions died.

A prominent Richmond physician, Dr. James B. McCaw, was put in charge of this unprecedented institution. McCaw had to solve innumerable problems to keep such a large institution running under deteriorating wartime conditions. A nearby farm, "Tree Hill," was obtained on loan. The cows and goats raised there provided meat and milk (the soldiers delighted in kid meat), and produce raised there provided food or was used for barter. A canal boat, *The Chimborazo*, traveled up the James River as far as Lexington and Lynchburg to obtain food by bartering yarn from cotton grown on the farm and shoes produced in hospital shops from the skins of animals used for meat. The hospital bakery produced 7,000 to 10,000 loaves a day, and the grease from its five great soup kitchens was mixed with lye that had been brought through the blockade to make soap. Many Confederate hospitals also set up bakeries that were larger than they needed. They traded the excess bread to the local populace in exchange for food items that the hospital needed. Convalescent soldiers, mostly recovering wounded, and volunteers did most of the work in the shops, bakeries, and gardens.[30,31] Union hospitals also traded their surplus supplies and food for other necessities or delicacies. Many hospitals on both sides organized their own gardens to provide vegetables.

Over the course of the war, a total of six massive permanent hospital complexes were built in and around Richmond, providing a total of over 20,000 beds.[32] One of them, the Winder Hospital, was about the same size as Chimborazo or possibly even larger. Winder opened with a bed capacity of 3,000, which quickly grew to at least 4,300 beds, divided into five divisions, with an additional tent division. Soldiers were assigned according to their home state. The

A shack, taken from Chimborazo Hospital after the war and used as living quarters by an African-American named Braxton Howard. It was moved to downtown Richmond where it was photographed on March 25, 1900.

hospital had ninety-eight buildings, including a huge bakery, warehouses, employees' barracks, a library, and bathhouses. Like Chimborazo, it was also located near the James River and had two canal boats, which it used to barter food grown on its own 125-acre farm.

The Spottswood Hotel in Richmond was used as a hospital. A number of Confederate generals met in the parlor of the Spottswood Hotel on July 13, 1861, to discuss troop dispositions before the impending Battle of Manassas (Bull Run). The basement of the hotel was used as the Lanier Hospital. It opened on July 2, 1862, to care for the enormous numbers of casualties sustained during the previous month when the Seven Days Battles of the Peninsula Campaign were fought.

Located in the area of Richmond, Virginia, the Howard's Grove Hospital had 1,150 beds in 1864 before it was temporarily closed because of the difficulties of maintaining it late in the war. Patients were transferred primarily to the Jackson and Chimborazo Hospitals, but the hospital continued to function after the war.

Picture of the Spottswood Hotel on Main Street in Richmond, on an envelope mailed to Alexander Hamilton Stephens, Vice-President of the Confederate States of America, addressed to his home in Crawfordville, Georgia. The envelope was postmarked Lynchburg, Virginia, and cost 10 cents to mail. (From the collection of F. Terry Hambrecht, M.D.)

Howard's Grove Hospital.

SPECIALTY HOSPITALS

Developments in medical sciences led to the establishment of civilian specialty hospitals in the United States, beginning in the 1850s. Hospitals devoted to eye and ear diseases appeared in New York and Boston. A Federal military hospital, the Desmarres Hospital, "especially set apart for diseases of the eye and ear," was established in Washington in 1863. (On August 23, 1864, it was moved to Chicago.) The 150-bed hospital was headed by Surgeon J. H. Hildreth, of the U.S. Volunteers, who did eye and throat operations;[33] tonsillectomies also were performed there.[34,35] Near the end of the war, the Confederate Army opened an eye hospital in Athens, Georgia, under the command of Surgeon Bolling A. Pope.[36]

A special hospital devoted to the study of nerve injuries among Civil War soldiers was established in Philadelphia. The Turner's Lane Hospital was headed by Dr. S. Weir Mitchell, who became one of the initial leaders of the field of neurology in the United States. Mitchell and his coworkers described many previously unknown syndromes, resulting from peripheral nerve injuries, that served to delineate the function of specific nerves. They described facial nerve paralysis and abnormalities resulting from wounds of various autonomic nerves, such as reflex sympathetic dystrophy and Horner's syndrome. They also described the syndrome of causalgia, including the now well-known phantom limb syndrome. The book based on their observations, *Gunshot Wounds and Other Injuries of Nerves*, is considered a classic.[37] The hospital was also the site of original observations on heart disease, including Dr. Jacob M. DaCosta's description of psychogenic cardiac symptoms, called "soldier's heart."[38]

Orthopedic problems dominated the surgical scene, and special facilities were established to care for patients with fractures that would not heal (non-union), false joints (unhealed fracture sites that developed motion similar to a joint), and chronic dislocations. Two such Confederate hospitals were opened, one in Richmond, Virginia, and one in Lauderdale Springs, Mississippi. Hospitals for soldiers needing artificial limbs, unofficially known as "stump hospitals," were opened on both sides.[39]

HOSPITAL STEWARDS

In the tiny prewar regular army, pharmacists were appointed as hospital stewards, but during the war there were too few trained pharmacists available. Late in 1862, the Surgeon General asked Joseph Woodward to prepare *Hospital Steward's Manual: For the Instruction of Hospital Stewards, Ward-Masters, and Attendants, in Their Several Duties*. This volume explained the duties and functions of hospital stewards and was the training manual for soldiers appointed to these posts. The number of hospital stewards reached a total of about 700 at one point. They had a distinctive uniform, as shown in some of the following pictures. They were given the rank of noncommissioned officers (usually sergeant).

In the field, among the volunteer regiments, the regimental surgeon usually appointed a man from among the ranks to serve as a steward, training him in his duties with the help of Woodward's manual.

Hospital steward Henry M. Beer, 23rd Ohio.

Hospital steward Hennessy who served in a Philadelphia hospital.

In the general hospitals, a hospital steward usually served as the hospital administrator. All of the hospital personnel except the surgeons reported to him, including the wardmasters, nurses (male and female), cooks, and laundresses. Hospitals of over 150 beds were authorized to have more than one steward. The steward was also supposed to serve as a pharmacist, compounding prescriptions, keeping the hospital dispensary in order, and maintaining all of the supplies, including the surgical equipment.

In the field, when the army was on the move, transporting medicines without the containers being broken yet having them available when needed was a major problem. Hospital stewards were put in charge of mobile medicine wagons; in 1862. The army devised a light medicine wagon that traveled with the ambulances and carried a large supply of medicines. A later modification, the Autenrieth wagon, adopted in 1864, had increased storage space, allowing drugs to be stored in drawers and cabinets. This protected the contents from jostling when the ambulance was on the move and provided better accessibility to the medicines when the doors were opened. A hospital steward made these medicines available to the regimental surgeon during sick call and for treatment of casualties after a battle.

Unidentified hospital steward, Union Army, showing the typical dress uniform, including frock coat, sash and sword.

A picture dated 1863 of hospital steward James Nebrich, of the Headquarters unit of the 2nd Division, 5th Army Corps.

Hospital steward James W. Steele, 46th Illinois.

Hospital steward Charles McQueston, 6th Maine, wearing a short white coat.

Salt print of hospital steward Charp of the Army of the Potomac.

Framed tintype of Hospital Steward Isaac G. Cole who served after the Battle of Antietam at Locust Spring Hospital. The Locust Spring Hospital was established near the left end of the Union line at Antietam, behind the 5th Corps. The surgeon in charge was T. H. Squires, from the 89th NY Volunteers.

A hand-tinted CDV of an unidentified hospital steward.

Unidentified hospital steward wearing frock coat and sash; note the Medical Department hat device on his cap.

Hospital steward Palmer Roberts; notice the 6th Corps badge on his hat.

ENDNOTES

1 Mitchell, S.W., On the Medical Department in the Civil War. Address to Physicians' Club of Chicago, February 25, 1913, *Journal of the American Medical Association.* 1914; 52:1445–1450.

2 Greenbie, M. L. B., *Lincoln's Daughters of Mercy.* New York: G. P. Putnam's Sons, 1944, p. 70.

3 *Medical and Surgical History,* Part 3, Vol. 1, p. 898.

4 Gillette, *The United States Army Medical Department,* 1818–1865, p. 290.

5 Greenbie, *Lincoln's Daughters of Mercy,* p. 135.

6 Blaisdell, F. W., Medical Advances during the Civil War. *Archives of Surgery.* 1988 Sept; 123(9):1045.

7 Mitchell, pp. 1445–1450.

8 Nightingale, F., *Notes on Nursing and Notes on Hospitals.* London: Harrison, 1859. (Repub.: Birmingham, Ala.: Classics of Medicine Library, 1982.).

9 Gillette, pp. 230, 251, 290.

10 Roberts, D. J., in Appendix D of *Photographic History of the Civil War,* Vol. 4B, p. 349.

11 Records of Adjutant General's Office. National Archives and Records Administration, Washington, D.C., RG94, Entry #626.

12 Roberts, D. J. In: *The Photographic History of the Civil War.* New York: Review of Reviews, 1970 (orig. pub. 1911), Vol. 4B.

13 National Archives and Records Administration, RG94, Entry #626.

14 Burdette, H. C., *Hospitals and Asylums of the World.* London: Churchill, 1891–3. Quoted in: Freemon, F. R., *Microbes and Minie Balls: An Annotated Bibliography of Civil War Medicine.* Rutherford, N.J.: Fairleigh Dickinson Univ. Press, 1993, p. 160.

15 *Medical and Surgical History of the War of the Rebellion,* First Surgical volume, p. 937.

16 Ibid., p 910.

17 Ibid., p 913.

18 Ibid., p 913.

19 *Medical and Surgical History,* Part 3, Vol, 1, p. 910. On the General Hospitals, report of J. S. Billings, Part 3, Vol. 1, p. 898.

20 *Medical and Surgical History,* Part 3, Vol. 1, pp. 940–942.

21 *Medical and Surgical History,* Part 3, Vol. 1, p. 927.

22 Greenbie, *Lincoln's Daughters of Mercy,* p. 166. Also in: Oates, *A Woman of Valor: Clara Barton and the Civil War.*

23 Poem: "Barbara Frietchie" (1864), by John Greenleaf Whittier; play: *Barbara Frietchie* (1899), by Clyde Fitch.

24 Sherman, W. T., October 29, 1862. *O.R. Series I,* Vol. XVII/2 Art. 25 p. 856.

25 *Medical and Surgical History,* Part 3, Vol. 1, p. 917.

26 Newton University Hospital, Baltimore, *Medical and Surgical History,* Part 3, Vol. 1, p. 962.

27 Wheat, Tl Al Receiving and Forwarding Hospitals of the Army of Northern Virginia, Presentation at 5th Annual Conference of the Society of Civil War Surgeons, Knoxville, Tenn., March 21, 1998.

28 Records from the Winder Hospital at the National Archives and Records Administration and the Lake City Florida General Hospital at The Eleanor S. Brockenbrough LI-brary, Museum of the Confederacy, Richmond, Va.

29 Roberts, D. J., op. cit., p. 349.

30 Bill, A. H., *The Beleaguered City: Richmond 1861–65.* New York: A. A. Knopf, 1946.

31 Greenbie, *Lincoln's Daughters of Mercy.*

32 Waitt, R. W., *Confederate Military Hospitals in Richmond*. Richmond: Richmond Civil War Centennial Committee, 1964. Also in: Roberts, *Photographic History of the Civil War,* Vol. 4B, p. 292.

33 *Medical and Surgical History,* Surgical Section, Vol. 1, pp. 385–6, 419; Medical Section, Vol. 3, p. 961.

34 Hospital Register, National Archives and Records Administration, RG94, Stack area 9W3, Row 3, Compartment 2.

35 *Medical and Surgical History,* Medical Section, Vol. 3, p. 896.

36 Cunningham, H. H., *Doctors in Gray: The Confederate Medical Service.* Baton Rouge, La.: Louisiana State Univ. Press, 1958, p. 215.

37 Mitchell, S. W., Morehouse, G. R., and Keen, W. W., *Gunshot Wounds and Other Injuries of Nerves.* Philadelphia: Lippincott, 1864 (Republished San Francisco: Norman Pub. Co., 1989).

38 DaCosta, J. M., On Irritable Heart. *American Journal of Medical Sciences.* 1871; 61:17.

39 Hospital Register, National Archives and Records Administration. RG94, Stack area 9W3, Row 3, Compartment 2.

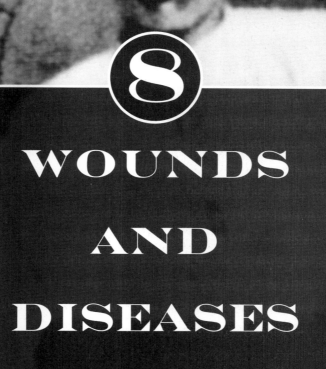

8

WOUNDS

AND

DISEASES

DURING THE CIVIL WAR the carnage was enormously appalling. More than 600,000 deaths occurred, more than in all of the United States' other wars combined, and an unknown total of the wounded were left with permanent injuries and disabilities. The photographic record of these phenomena indelibly reminds us of the cost of war and the intense devotion and patriotism of those who fought and kept on fighting for four years despite the carnage.

The Medical Department of the Union Army purposely set out to record and analyze the soldiers' experiences during the course of the war, with the aim of learning as much as possible from the terrible events of the war. As part of their record keeping, physicians, primarily those working in the Union Surgeon General's Office, used the new methods of photography. Photographs of Civil War soldiers were taken to show their injuries, often showing the results of amputations; "empty sleeves" were common. Follow-up pictures of surviving wounded soldiers were also obtained after the war, some over a decade later. When combined with the records of professional photographers who accompanied the troops and arranged for posed photographs of battlefield casualties and important events, including some actual surgical procedures, we have a considerable amount of visual information about the carnage and suffering of the time.

Although two-thirds of the deaths of soldiers were caused by disease, sick patients in hospitals did not attract photographers. Physicians performed autopsies on a large proportion of the deaths in an attempt to learn as much as possible, and they used photography as well as drawings and paintings to show the anatomical effects of disease and the results of battlefield injuries. They even used the newly invented techniques of tissue staining for microscopic examinations and set up devices to do photomicrography, some of the earliest examples of that technology.

Many myths arose about the functioning of the Medical Departments of both sides during the war. These were generated in part by horror at the human suffering, which was mainly due to the poor performance of the medical staffs at the beginning of the war. Public press did not reflect the improvements in care during the course of the war, nor the accomplishments of the Civil War surgeons compared to their European contemporaries. The photographic record helps dispel some of those enduring misconceptions.

ANESTHESIA

By the time of the Civil War, anesthesia, which was originally introduced late in 1846, was almost completely accepted. Few surgeons still argued that the depressive effect of anesthesia increased the dangers of surgery, as many had during the Crimean War of 1854–56. Union Army surgeons used anesthesia approximately 80,000 times, and there is a record of failure to use it in exactly 254 cases, all occurring after the Battle of Iuka on September 19, 1862. No reasons were given why anesthetics were not administered in those cases. Confederate surgeons used anesthetics with similar consistency, although there probably were more instances of failure to use it because supplies ran out.

Chloroform was used about three-quarters of the time, and ether or a combination of the two in the remainder of the cases. Chloroform was preferred in the field because it was not flammable, smaller quantities were needed for each case, making transportation of it less of a problem, and its onset of action was quicker. As one surgeon reported, "From the rapidity of its effects, and from the small quantity required—qualities which can only be appreciated at their proper values by the field surgeon when surrounded by hundreds of wounded anxiously awaiting speedy relief—chloroform was preferred by nearly all the field surgeons, and their testimony as to its value and efficacy is almost unanimous, although all recommend the greatest care in its administration."[1]

Although chloroform was usually used in field hospitals, ether was preferred in the fixed general hospitals where the volume of anesthetic needed, the time of onset, and the problem of flammability were not issues. Surgeons were aware that ether was safer, but they had few fatalities from the chloroform because they used so little. Surgeons still worked as rapidly as possible—as they had before anesthesia became available—and the anesthetic was stopped promptly, often before the surgeon was entirely finished, because it did not wear off immediately.

The anesthetic was given by dropping it onto a folded cloth held over a patient's face or through a small device held over the mouth and nose. Several devices that diminished the evaporation of the anesthetic gas were invented to improve the administration of the anesthetic, especially among Confederate forces, for whom limited supplies stimulated conservation.

In addition to its use in major surgical procedures, anesthesia was given when wound treatments were going to be painful. The most notable example was the treatment of hospital gangrene with bromine, which came into widespread use in the last two years of the war. The bromine solution was used to irrigate the wound and saturate the margins of the gangrenous area, a very painful procedure. This treatment was uniformly done with general anesthesia, usually ether, because the procedure was performed in hospitals.[2] Anesthesia was also used in the treatment of tetanus in an attempt to relieve the painful, persistent muscle spasms, but it could not prevent the usual fatal outcome of that disease.

WOUND INFECTIONS, HOSPITAL GANGRENE, AND ERYSIPELAS

Virtually all wounds became infected in these pre-Listerian days. Everything about Civil War soldiers was dirty, including medical equipment, and wounds were always contaminated. Of course, at the time, bacteria were not understood to be the causes of disease; poisonous "miasmas" were thought to be the culprit, spread primarily through the air and acting chemically, like enzymes. That is why diseases now known as infectious were classified as "zymotic" at the time and why the Greek word for "poison," *virus*, was sometimes used to describe the agents. Contaminating dirty material (bits of clothing, grass, soil) and devital-ized tissue, all of which promote bacterial growth, were removed by surgeons, but not very thoroughly—partly for lack of time under the pressures of caring for so many wounded men and partly for lack of decent lighting.

As a result, suppuration, or the formation of pus, was almost universal. Surgeons some-times called the pus "laudable," not because they thought formation of pus was good, but as a description of the prognostic implication of the type of pus that formed. They called pus "laudable" when it was of the thick, creamy kind that usually stayed localized and was unlikely to spread and cause pyemia, or blood poisoning, with a fatal outcome. What was laudable about it was the likely outcome, and it was distinguished from "malignant pus," which was thin, bloody, and more likely to spread and lead to pyemia. In fact, pus with the qualities called "laudable" was mostly caused by staphylococci; the malignant type of pus was mostly caused by streptococci.

Two of the most severe and often fatal surgical infections were "hospital gangrene" and erysipelas (both primarily streptococcal infections). They often spread relentlessly, leading quickly to a fatal outcome. Erysipelas, officially called "traumatic erysipelas,"[3] starts super-ficially in the skin, although it usually requires some break in the skin for the organisms to gain a foothold. It begins with redness, tenderness, and other manifestations of inflammation. The infection may remain relatively localized, but it can spread swiftly beneath the skin, destroying tissues deeply and widely. It often spreads to local lymph nodes that drain the area and from there into the blood stream, the process that Civil War doctors called "pyemia," "septicemia," or "blood poisoning." Once spreading begins via the blood, organisms set up new sites of infection in a variety of tissues, in particular on heart valves, in the lungs, and often in the nervous system, where meningitis can develop. These complications were indeed frequently observed and well described by Civil War surgeons; they accounted for the high mortality rate of that disease.

The main cause of "hospital gangrene" was an aggressive bacterial infection, probably most often streptococcal. It spread in the hospitals and was rarely seen outside of hospitals. Civil War surgeons were aware of the communicability of these infections, even if they did not know that the cause was bacterial. Whenever possible, they isolated patients with either hospital gangrene or erysipelas in tents separate from the other patients and put these two types of patients together. They were aware of the relationship between the two conditions. They observed, for example, that a nurse handling a patient with hospital gangrene sometimes developed erysipelas in areas that had touched the gangrenous tissue.

Hospital gangrene rarely occurred in the field hospitals or in the larger, temporary general hospitals set up in tents near the battlefields. The disease was seen primarily in the relatively permanent hospitals in cities. Once it appeared, the infection spread from patient to patient or from patient to nurse. This phenomenon was called "hospitalism" in the nineteenth century; today it is termed "nosocomial infection" (using the Greek word for "hospital"). Because it was rarely seen outside of hospitals, the common name "hospital gangrene" was appropriate indeed.

Hospital gangrene caused widespread tissue death (gangrene), mostly because of clotting in the small arteries that supply blood to the tissues. A famous Philadelphia physician who had been a Civil War surgeon, S. Weir Mitchell, described the fearsome rate of development of the lesions of hospital gangrene as follows:

> A slight flesh wound began to show a gray edge of slough, and within two hours we saw this widening at the rate of half an inch an hour, and deepening. . . . Instant removal to open air tents, etherization, savage cautery with pure nitric acid or bromin [sic], and dressings of powdered charcoal enabled us to deal with these cases more or less well, but the mortality was hideous—at least 45 per cent.[4]

Various treatments being tried for hospital gangrene were evaluated in a notable clinical trial carried out by Union Surgeon Middleton Goldsmith. Goldsmith, who had been a medical school professor before the war, compared the survival rates of groups of patients with hospital gangrene who were treated with bromine, nitric acid, and other antiseptic agents, including iodine and carbolic acid. Goldsmith obtained clearly superior results using solutions of bromine applied to the surface and injected deeply into affected areas (usually with the patient under general anesthesia). In his report to the Surgeon General, he concluded, "Testimony of these cases will establish the value of bromine in hospital gangrene sufficiently at least for the purpose of challenging investigation."[5] Although a century later most clinical trials were conducted using carefully controlled double-blind studies of randomly assigned cases, the comparative method with statistical analyses used by Goldsmith remained the standard for the best clinical research for a long time after the Civil War.

Some Civil War surgeons reported that deaths from hospital gangrene had been entirely eliminated in their hospital as a result of the use of bromine and other agents. Others remained skeptical, apparently considering the treatment a fad.[6] According to data in the *Medical and Surgical History*, hospital gangrene was rare in the first year of the war, but it increased markedly in frequency during the second and third years. It decreased considerably in the last year and became rare shortly afterward; treatment with bromine and other antiseptic agents may have been responsible.

Civil War surgeons used the term "antiseptic." They called the tissue death that occurs in infections such as hospital gangrene "sepsis," a Greek term meaning putrefaction. They equated the tissue necrosis to the decay that occurs postmortem. Any agent that decreased the amount of tissue death, or sepsis, was thus an "antiseptic."

Hospital gangrene remained a major problem in Europe after it became infrequent in the United States. After the Franco-Prussian War (1870–71), a Munich hospital recorded that hospital gangrene and erysipelas attacked 80 percent of all wounds; it was so common that "its occurrence could be regarded as normal."[7]

AMPUTATIONS

After battles, the main job of surgeons was to stop bleeding, debride (clean away dead tissue and foreign material) and sew up superficial wounds, and splint fractures. Amputations were the main form of major surgery; the abdomen, chest, and head were invaded only under the most desperate of circumstances and rarely with a successful outcome. Diseases such as appendicitis and typhoid fever with peritonitis from a perforated bowel generally were not diagnosed during life and went untreated during that era. Even in civilian life, major surgery was mainly in the form of amputations, even after anesthesia was adopted.

Almost 30,000 amputations were recorded by Union surgeons, undoubtedly an incomplete number because it does not include those performed in hospitals as revisions of previous treatments, surgeries performed after men were discharged, or those that were simply not recorded, particularly during the early chaos. Although records are less complete, a similar number of amputations probably were done by Confederate surgeons. Photographs of Civil War soldiers taken to show their injuries frequently showed their remaining stumps.

Because lighting conditions were better outside, surgery was performed outdoors using daylight whenever possible. Soldiers who were passing by were dismayed by the piles of amputated extremities lying near the improvised operating tables. They also saw several assistants holding writhing patients onto the operating table, and heard moaning and groaning. This led to the impression that anesthesia was not being used. Actually, it was in use, but the superficial depth of the anesthesia that was common during the Civil War—to avoid deaths that would have occurred from chloroform if it had been used to obtain a deeper level of anesthesia—put the patient into an excited phase, capable of making loud noises and uncontrolled muscular motions that required restraint. Many autobiographies of participants in the Civil War include descriptions of such gory, tumultuous scenes. Letters home frequently described their observations and the implication that the patients were in pain because of poor anesthesia but no letter has been found in which a soldier actually said he had pain during the surgery—though they do record a great deal of pain before and after. The widely held idea that anesthesia was rarely used and the criticism of the large number of amputations generated considerable disparagement at the time. These notions have persisted to a considerable extent ever since.

Amputations were usually performed because of the devastating tissue destruction produced by the main type of ammunition used during the war, Minié balls. They flew with relatively low velocity, often tumbling as they moved, ripping up the tissues and usually shattering any bones they struck.[8] Badly torn up, contaminated tissues virtually always became infected. Because the

"Amputation being performed in a hospital tent at Gettysburg, July 1863." (National Archives and Records Administration 79-T-2265.)

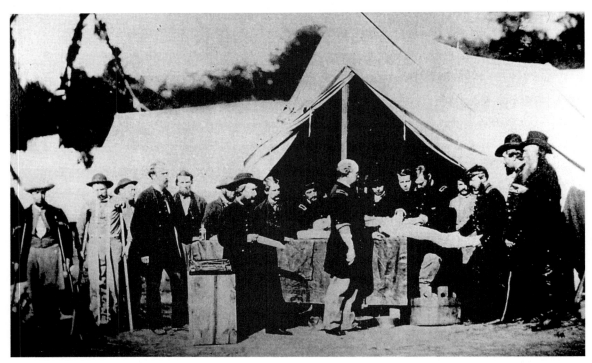

Another "amputation scene at Gettysburg." (Courtesy of the U.S. Army Medical History Institute, Carlisle, PA.)

missiles broke through the skin, carrying in dirty material from the skin and clothing, the fractures were defined as "compound," and the bones, smashed into many fragments, were termed "comminuted." (These terms are still used with the same meaning.) Compound, comminuted fractures provide an excellent milieu for growth of bacteria, and the bone itself, along with its marrow, usually became infected. Osteomyelitis did not respond to treatment available at the time; before the days of antibiotics, and the condition frequently lasted for the rest of the patient's life.

Surgeons could delay the decision to amputate, but when they performed "secondary amputations"—a term usually used for amputations done forty-eight hours or more after the injury—infection had time to gain a foothold and start to spread. Cutting through infected tissues enhances the spread of infection, often allowing it to gain access to and disseminate through the blood stream. Civil War surgeons knew this fact too, from observation and experience, although they did not know that bacteria were responsible. The result of such dissemination, "blood poisoning," or "septicemia" carried a 99 percent fatality rate. In deciding whether to amputate, most Civil War surgeons were guided by the aphorism "Every hour the humane operation [of amputation] is delayed diminishes the chance of a favorable issue."[9] (In many ways, this idea parallels the modern concept of the "golden hour" for trauma patients.) Civil War surgeons knew that delayed amputations during the Crimean War had resulted in greater mortality than those performed immediately, and they kept the British experience in mind.

Judging from civilian experience, a mortality rate of approximately 50 percent was expected if amputations were delayed over forty-eight hours. Of the total of 29,980 amputations recorded on Union soldiers, the mortality rate was 26.3 percent. Figures are not as complete for the Confederate Army, but the available data for survival are almost identical to those of the Union.[10] The mortality rate following amputation varied with the location on the body: the further the amputation was from the torso, the better was the final outcome.

The mortality rate for amputations among the soldiers was about half that reported from civilian hospitals. A major reason for this discrepancy undoubtedly was the rapid evacuation of wounded soldiers, after the ambulance system was instituted, and a prepared surgical team that made the decision to perform amputations early. Among civilians, there was usually greater delay in performing the surgery.

The enormous amount of criticism of Civil War surgeons received during and after the war for performing too many amputations forms the main impression that most people have when the subject of Civil War medicine arises. Yet surgeons who were there, looking back years later, felt that they had, in fact, performed too few amputations rather than too many. As Dr. William Williams Keen, a prominent late nineteenth-century surgeon (who had served as a medical cadet during the Civil War) has said, "Far more lives were lost from refusal to amputate than by amputating."[11]

The two photographs on page 170, identified as amputation scenes at Gettysburg, in fact show preliminaries to the actual amputation. In both, the operating surgeon can be seen standing with his knife ready but not in use. Other surgeons are examining the patient. These pictures illustrate the controls that were, in fact, established by late 1862 because of accusations that surgeons were performing excessive numbers of amputations, and operating on mildly injured soldiers just to gain experience.

The procedure illustrated here was inaugurated in the Army of the Potomac by Medical Director Jonathan Letterman in the fall of 1862 and is recorded in his book, *Medical Reminiscences of the Army of the Potomac* as follows:

> There will be selected from the division . . . three medical officers, who will be the operating staff of the hospital, upon whom will rest the immediate responsibility for the performance of all important operations. In all doubtful cases they will consult together, and a majority of them shall decide upon the expediency and character of the operation. These officers will be selected from the division without regard to rank, but *solely* on account of their known prudence, judgment and skill. The Surgeon-in-Chief of the division is enjoined to be especially careful in the selection of these officers, choosing only those who have distinguished themselves for surgical skill, sound judgment, and conscientious regard for the highest interests of the wounded.[12] [Italics in the original.]

This system was put into effect widely in both the Union and Confederate armies, although, on the Confederate side, restricted manpower usually limited the decision to that of a single consulting surgeon. In all cases, the surgeon who performed the operation was selected for his skill, but it was another surgeon or a board of three surgeons, selected primarily for their judgment, who made the decision as to whether an amputation was to be performed. It is also described in General Order No. 19 of the 18th Corps of the Army of the Potomac, issued May 20, 1864:

> All cases of amputation must either be first designated for operation by the surgeon in charge of the hospital, or be determined upon by a majority vote of a board of at least 3 surgeons to be detailed by the surgeon in charge, or the corps medical director.[13]

It is most noteworthy that the selection of the individuals described in this order, as in Letterman's description of his system, was to be based *solely* on ability "without regard to rank." This is a notable departure from the standard army principle, "Rank has its privileges."

A passage in the prime textbook of surgery used during the war by Confederate surgeons, written by Professor Chisolm of Charleston, explains the need for such regulations and describes the actions taken in the Southern armies to correct the problem:

> Among a certain class of surgeons . . . amputations have often been performed when limbs could have been saved, and the amputating knife has often been brandished, by inexperienced surgeons, over simple flesh wounds. In the beginning of the war the desire for operating was so great among the large number of medical officers recently from the schools, who were for the first time in a position to indulge this extravagant propensity, that the limbs of soldiers were in as much danger from the ardor of young surgeons as from the missiles of the enemy.

In the next paragraph, Chisolm added:

> It was for this reason that, in the distribution of labor in the field infirmaries, it was recommended that the surgeon who had the greatest experience, and upon whose judgment the greatest reliance could be placed, should officiate as examiner, and his decision be carried out by those who may possess a greater facility or desire for the operative manual.[14]

This passage appeared in the third edition of Chisolm's book, published in 1863. It describes the problem of excessive numbers of amputations that existed on both sides early in the war, which generated so much criticism of the medical departments. The reputation of the surgeons never recovered from these criticisms, despite the corrective actions that were taken and the overall superior record of their performance compared to European military surgeons in both the Crimean War (1854–56) and the Franco-Prussian War (1870–71).

PHOTOGRAPHS OF WOUNDED SOLDIERS

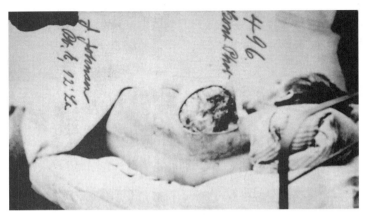

Wound of upper back, probably with fractured scapula and secondary infection, which look like hospital gangrene.

The soldier shown above is Jacob Johnson, 12th Louisiana (Confederate States of America). He fought in General John Bell Hood's Confederate Army and was wounded at the Battle of Franklin, November 30, 1864. He was cared for by the Union Army Medical Department and was treated at Hospital Number 1, Nashville, Tennessee. [Case 12231].

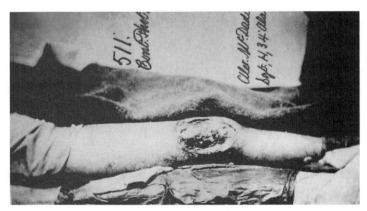

Hospital gangrene of leg.

The patient shown above is Alex M. Dade, a sergeant in Company H, 34th Alabama and a member of General Hood's army. He sustained a gunshot flesh wound on the right thigh just above the knee, at the Battle of Nashville, December 16, 1864, and was cared for by the Union Army. Dade was admitted to Hospital Number 1 in Nashville, Tennessee on December 17, 1864. Hospital gangrene developed on December 20, and he was treated with bromine on December 26.

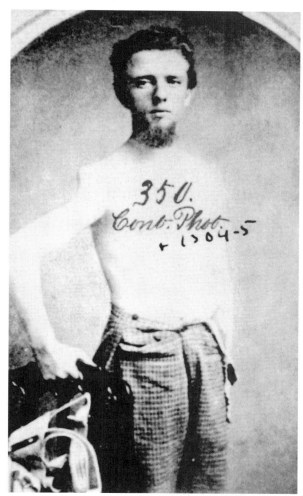

*Unidentified wounded soldier showing results of resection
of part of the humerus.*

Resection of part of the long bone of an extremity was performed to avoid amputation. The lack of continuity of the bone structure, as occurred in the soldier in the photograph above, usually resulted in a "flail" arm, which could be moved but not be well controlled. Note how the upper end of his arm lies below the normal level of the shoulder joint. The soldier is bracing his arm on a chair, which may have been necessary to hold the arm away from the body in order to show the result of the surgery. However, it was common in the 1850s for people being photographed to brace themselves in some fashion on a chair or other object in order to remain still and allow for the long exposure necessary with the photographic techniques of the era.

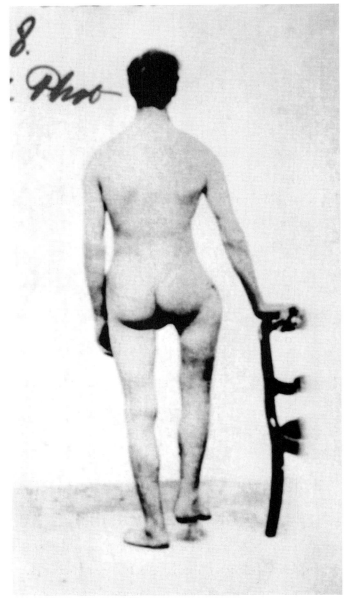

Corporal E. Worthen, Co. B, 2d Vermont, age 25 years, was wounded in the right thigh, at the Wilderness, May 5, 1864.

A detailed history of Corporal Worthen's care is available: The wound was caused by a Minié ball, which entered the thigh in front, passed directly through and emerged posteriorly, at the lower border of the glutei muscles (in the buttocks), comminuting the femur for about three inches. There were great delays in moving the wounded after the battles at the Wilderness and Spottsylvania, but it is not clear how much that affected his care. Worthen was evacuated to the hospital of the 2nd division, 6th Corps, at Fredericksburg, and then to the army's port facility (Aquia Landing), where men and supplies could be ferried north on the Potomac River. He arrived at a hospital at Alexandria three weeks after his injury. While hospitalized, Worthen developed typhoid fever and erysipelas. The wound kept draining pus from the entry and exit sites, and a fragment of bone was removed in July, 1864; subsequently, about fifty pieces of bone were removed via these sites.

About nine months later, March 17, 1865, he was transferred to Sloan Hospital, Montpelier, Vermont, near his home. When he arrived there, the wound continued to discharge pus, but he could get around on crutches. The fractures became firmly united and he could walk a short distance without crutch or cane, but the injured limb was described as shortened by two and one-half inches and considerably deformed. Surgeon C. L. Allen, of Rutland, Vermont, wrote on September 24, 1866:

> The right limb is now three inches shorter than the left. An opening (the wound
> of entrance) still exists in front of the trochanter, into which a probe passes about four
> inches; another opening posteriorly (the wound of exit) allows the probe to pass in
> about three inches. A third opening exists near the middle of the inside of the thigh,
> having been made by the Surgeon for the discharge of the burrowing pus.

When Dr. Allen was called to visit Worthen four years later, on October 23, 1870, he found him "suffering from pyaemia, resulting from the wound breaking out anew, from the effects of which he died October 25, 1870."[15]

This unfortunate soldier's case illustrates the persisting illness that was typical of the osteomyelitis that followed contaminated fractures. In that era, before antibiotics, there was a continuous threat that the infection could spread and lead to "pyemia" and death. In Corporal Worthen's case, this outcome occurred more than six years after the injury. In the interval, he was constantly sick, in pain, and draining foul pus; he had a deformed, shortened leg that limited his mobility. A successful amputation with a prosthetic artificial leg would have been a much better outcome, but amputation of the upper thigh and hip area carried a frightfully high likelihood of fatality, and he probably would not have survived the immediate postoperative period.

The following is excerpted from Sergeant E. D. Ulmer's case history, which was recorded in detail in the *Medical and Surgical History:*

CASE 333. Sergeant E. D. Ulmer, Co. G, 15th New Jersey, aged 21 years, was wounded at Cedar Creek, October 19, 1864, by a musket ball, which entered the inner face of the left thigh, fractured the bone, and lodged under the skin on the outer side of the limb. The femur was badly comminuted, fissures extending into the knee joint and upward for seven inches. The ball was extracted at a field hospital of the Sixth Corps, and it was determined to attempt to save the limb. The wounded man was conveyed to Baltimore, to Jarvis Hospital, on October 24th. Intense arthritis supervened, with deep dissecting abscesses in the thigh. On November 14th haemorrhage to the extent of twenty-five ounces took place from both orifices, which were in a sloughing condition. The patient was put under ether, and amputation at the middle of the thigh was performed by Acting Assistant Surgeon Edmund. G. Waters. The patient rallied promptly after the operation, and in a few weeks was able to get about on crutches. Yet the stump continued painful, and the extremity of the femur was found to be necrosed. In March, 1865, it was found that a cylindrical sequestrum [fragment of dead bone] was loose. This was removed, on March 8th, by Acting Assistant Surgeon B. B. Miles, with forceps. On May 29, 1865, he was discharged.

On the following day he started for Philadelphia, and, unfortunately, on the journey he fell with violence upon the stump. After this there was increased suppuration, with deep-seated pain in the stump. On the 22d of January, 1866, fifteen months after the original injury, while dressing the part as usual, a haemorrhage occurred from one of the fistulous openings at the end of the stump, amounting, according to his statement, to at least a pint. On account of this haemorrhage, he was admitted into the Pennsylvania Hospital. The history of the case and the appearances of the stump clearly indicated the existence of osteo-myelitis . . . The risk of recurrence of dangerous haemorrhage, and the extensive disease of the femur, obviously demanded operative treatment. On February 17, 1866, in the hospital amphitheater, the patient being etherised, an exploratory operation was made by Dr. Thomas G. Morton, the attending surgeon, and amputation was decided upon by him in consultation with Drs. W. Hunt and D. H. Agnew. The abdominal tourniquet, used the first time in this country by Professor Joseph Pancoast, June, 1860, was applied, and

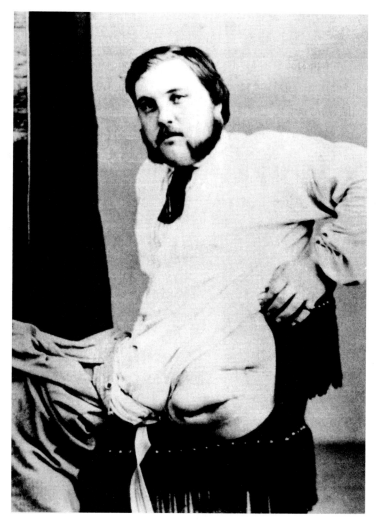

Large albumen print of First Sergeant Ulmer, who survived an amputa-tion of the upper thigh, a procedure that carried a high mortality rate.

antero-posterior integumentary flaps were dissected up; the femoral artery was then tied, the muscles cut circularly, and the head of the bone was disarticulated. The aorta was so completely controlled by the abdominal tourniquet that no arterial jet was observed during the operation. About sixteen ligatures were applied. The flaps were approximated with adhesive plaster, no sutures being deemed necessary. The dressings consisted of lint soaked in pure laudanum. The patient reacted well; under vigorous stimulating treatment and the local application of permanganate of potash he rapidly recovered. He left the hospital March 27, 1866.[16]

Unknown sergeant with wounded arm in sling.

The soldier in the photograph above apparently has a bloody stain on the dressing over his hand. He is surrounded by women, probably members of his family. The woman seated next to him seems also to have her arm in a sling and stains on her dress, suggesting that she has been injured also. There is probably an interesting story being documented by this picture, given that people made prior arrangements to pose for a photograph and thus would have had time to change their clothes, but we have no record of their story.

Tintypes of soldier with right arm missing and a second soldier standing with the aid of crutches. There is no other information available.

Unknown soldier with amputation below the knee, another holding crutches. No other information available.

Sgt. Alfred Stratton, 147th NY, wounded during the siege of Petersburg in 1864, requiring amputation of both arms. No other information is available.

Samuel Decker, 4th U.S. Artillery, age 24 (at time wound sustained), a double-arm amputee.

In 1867, Mr. Decker gave a statement for inclusion in the *Medical and Surgical History,* which is probably when this picture was taken. He said, in part, that he was injured at the Battle of Perryville, October 8, 1862. While ramming his piece during the battle, he had half of his right forearm and somewhat less of the left forearm blown off by the premature explosion of the gun. At the same time, his face and chest were badly burned. Five hours after the accident both forearms were amputated by the circular method, about the middle. He stayed in the field hospital at Perryville until the wounds were partially healed. On November 1 he was sent to Louisville, where he was discharged from the service. About the middle of January, 1863, the stumps were completely healed. In the autumn of 1864, Mr. Decker began to make experiments to try to provide himself with artificial limbs, and during the following March:

. . . he produced an apparatus hitherto unrivaled for its ingenuity and utility. . . . With the aid of this ingenious apparatus, he is enabled to write legibly, to pick up any small object, a pin for example, to carry packages of ordinary weight, and to feed and clothe himself. This pensioner has been for some years employed as a doorkeeper at the House of Representatives, and was still on duty there in March, 1876.

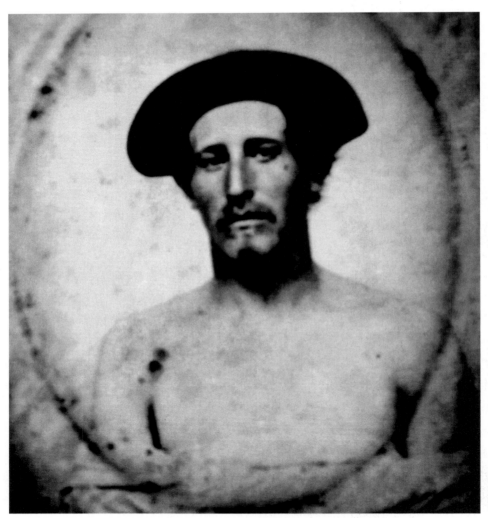

Unidentified soldier with bullet wound near right shoulder.

Unidentified soldier with healed wound of inner surface of left thigh.

Photo of a painting titled The Empty Sleeve. *The "child" in the soldier's lap, holding the sleeve open, is undoubtedly a manikin, a prop for such paintings and photographs. Note the sad but wistful look on the face of the unidentified soldier.*

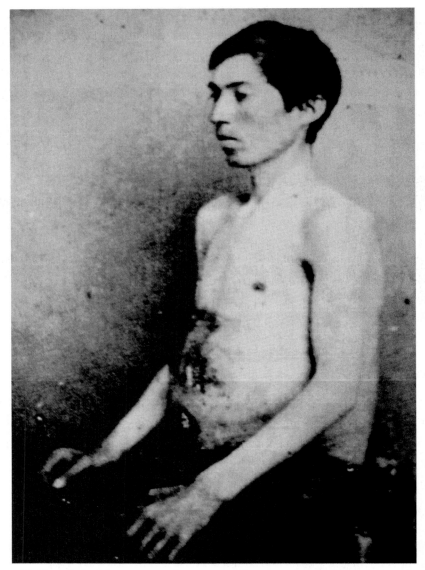

Unidentified soldier, apparently recovering from a serious abdominal wound.

The photograph above of an unidentified soldier shows distention of the soldier's abdomen, suggesting serious intra-abdominal pathology. The dark hemorrhage around the umbilicus is probably the result of intra-abdominal hemorrhage, and the discoloration above it is probably the result of trauma to the abdominal wall. It is unfortunate that a case history is not available, given that relatively few soldiers recovered from serious intra-abdominal wounds.

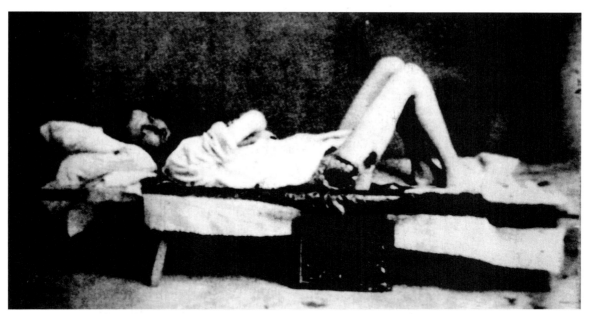

Unidentified soldier with large area of sloughing of skin following a wound in upper right leg, over the area of the hip joint.

There is no case history available about the man shown in the photograph above, but the appearance of the wound and the separate area of very dark discoloration below it on the thigh suggest that hospital gangrene had developed. A fatal outcome was frequent with this complication of a wound, but the outcome of this particular soldier's injury is not known.

Private Willis of the 3rd Rhode Island Volunteers, who had a resection of part of the left arm, probably a portion of the humerus. The arm seems straight but its functionality is not known.

Private Baker of the 23rd Ohio, who had a persistent, ulcerated wound of the left ankle. The appearance of the ulcer suggests localized hospital gangrene.

Photograph of a group of wounded, partially disabled veterans, taken at the Abraham Lincoln School for the Maimed, where training for new jobs was provided.

E.D. Bates, who apparently has multiple necrotic lesions of the buttocks, possibly the result of shrapnel. Because he seems well and is shown standing, Mr. Bates probably did not have hospital gangrene, despite the appearance of these lesions.

Private Reardon (shown in a photograph on the facing page) was admitted to the Armory Square Hospital in Washington, D.C. only one day following his injury. Surgeon D. W. Bliss, U.S. Volunteers, found that Reardon's right humerus was shattered by a fragment of shell, which was removed from its "lodgement" under the deltoid muscle, near the shoulder. The fragment was four inches long, one inch broad, and weighed nine ounces. Surgeon Bliss excised the head and six inches of the shaft of the humerus through a straight incision on the outside of the limb. His case was written up as illustrating retained mobility of the arm after excision. The arm was three inches shorter than the other, but muscle development was comparable. Reardon was able to move the arm in all directions except abduction (i.e., movement laterally, away from the body), as illustrated in the photograph, in which he has placed his arm on a support to hold it away from his body. He must have developed infection of the bone after the operation, because he expelled a segment of bone from the area where the sawing incision was made, but he apparently recovered and remained well thereafter.

After recovering in March 1866, Reardon was reenlisted and assigned to duty as an orderly in the Army Medical Museum (where most of these photos of convalescent wounded soldiers were taken). From that date until the time the picture was taken (March 1875), he served continuously, suffering very little inconvenience "from the mutilation he has undergone." The record of his case (Case 1529), went on to state that "Without difficulty he can place his right hand on the top of his head; he can lift a weight of two hundred pounds or more with the injured limb without pain. The movements of the forearm and hand are not in the least impaired, and there is great freedom of all the movements of the arm except abduction."[17] After the report of his case in *The Medical and Surgical History*, the article went on to discuss the factors that influenced the mobility and usefulness of an arm after excision of part of the humerus. For example, it stated that, "The amount of after-mobility in the limb appears to depend greatly upon the extent to which the nerve trunks and muscular attachments have been respected by the missile and by the knife, and upon the precautions taken in the after treatment."[18]

Private. John F. Reardon, 6th N.Y. Cavalry, whose right arm was wounded at Culpepper, Virginia on October 11, 1863.

Tintype of image of young Union soldier who lost both arms.

Tintype of Private Calvin Snyder of Wolcott, Vermont, who died of measles.

This picture was taken in 1861, "just before war," but clearly Private Snyder is already in uniform. Measles was particularly common in the first months of the war, often appearing as soon as soldiers were gathered into groups as part of the induction process. Because measles is usually a very severe infection in adults, frequently leading to pneumonia, it resulted in a considerable mortality rate (about 15 percent) among Civil War soldiers.

ENDNOTES

1   *(1) Circular* No. 6, War Department, Surgeon General's Office, Washington, November 1, 1865 (included in *Medical and Surgical History*, Part 3, Vol. 2, p. 888).

2   Weir, M. S., On the Medical Department in the Civil War. Address to Physicians' Club of Chicago, February 25, 1913, *Journal of the American Medical Association*. 1914; 52:1445–1450.

3   *Medical and Surgical History*, Surgical Section, Vol. 3, p. 851.

4   Mitchell, S. W., On the Medical Department in the Civil War. Address to Physicians' Club of Chicago, February 25, 1913, *Journal of the American Medical Association*. 1914; 52:1446.

5   *Medical and Surgical History*, Surgical Section, Vol. 3, p. 836.

6   Gillette, M. C., *The United States Army Medical Department, 1818–1865*, Washington, D.C.: Center of Military History, U.S. Army, 1987, pp. 281–3.

7   Walter, C. W., *The Aseptic Treatment of Wounds*. New York: Macmillan, 1948.

8   Howard, E. L., The Effects of Minié Balls on Bone. *Confederate States Medical and Surgical Journal*. 1864; 1:58. Also in: Sorrel, F., Gunshot Wounds in the Army of Northern Virginia. *Confederate States Medical and Surgical Journal*. 1864; 1:153.

9   Riley, *Medicine in the Confederacy*, Part I, p. 63. *Military Medicine* 121:53, 1956 (Jan.).

10 Sorrel, P. Gunshot Wounds, Army of Northern Virginia. *Confederate States Medical and Surgical Journal*. Oct. 1864; 1:154.

11 Keen, W. W., Surgical Reminiscences of the Civil War. *Transactions of the College of Physicians of Philadelphia*. 3rd Series, 1905; 27:95–114.

12 Letterman, J., *Medical Reminiscences of the Army of the Potomac*. Knoxville, Tenn.: Bohemian Brigade, 1994.

13 Official Records, General Orders No. 19 May 20, 1864.

14 Chisolm, J. J., *A Manual of Military Surgery for Use of the Surgeons in the Confederate Army*. 3rd ed. Columbia: Evans and Cogswell, 1864. Republished: Dayton, Ohio: Morningside Press, 1992, p. 409.

15 *Medical and Surgical History*, Part 3, Vol. 2, p. 183.

16 Ibid., p. 156.

17 *Medical and Surgical History*, Part 2, Vol. 2, p. 552.

18 Ibid., p. 658.

INDEX

Page numbers followed by an italicized *p* indicate reference to a photograph.